Chief Eneas Bigknife

Kootenai Indian Patriot and Diplomat

Chief Eneas Bigknife

Kootenai Indian Patriot and Diplomat

by Peter Ronan

edited by
Robert Bigart

published by
Salish Kootenai College Press
Pablo, Montana

distributed by
University of Nebraska Press
Lincoln, Nebraska

Cover design: Corky Clairmont, artist/graphic designer, Pablo, Montana.

Cover illustration: Chief Eneas Bigknife. Archives and Special Collections, Mansfield Library, University of Montana, Missoula, photo number 81-284

Library of Congress Cataloging-in-Publication Data:

Names: Ronan, Peter, 1839-1893 author | Bigart, Robert editor
Title: Chief Eneas Bigknife : Kootenai Indian patriot and diplomat / by Peter Ronan ; edited by Robert Bigart.
Description: Pablo, Montana : Salish Kootenai College Press, 2025. | Includes bibliographical references and index.
Identifiers: LCCN 2025016878 | ISBN 9781934594377 papeerback
Subjects: LCSH: Ronan, Peter, 1839-1893--Correspondence | Big Knife, Eneas. 1828-1900 | Kootenai Indians--Montana--Flathead Valley--History--19th century
Classification: LCC E99.K85 R66 2025 | DDC 978.6/820200497992--dc23/eng/20250515
LC record available at https://lccn.loc.gov/2025016878

ISBN 978-1-934594-37-7

Published by Salish Kootenai College Press, PO Box 70, Pablo, MT 59855.

Distributed by University of Nebraska Press, 1111 Lincoln Mall, Lincoln, NE 68588-0630, order 1-800-755-1105, www.nebraskapress.unl.edu.

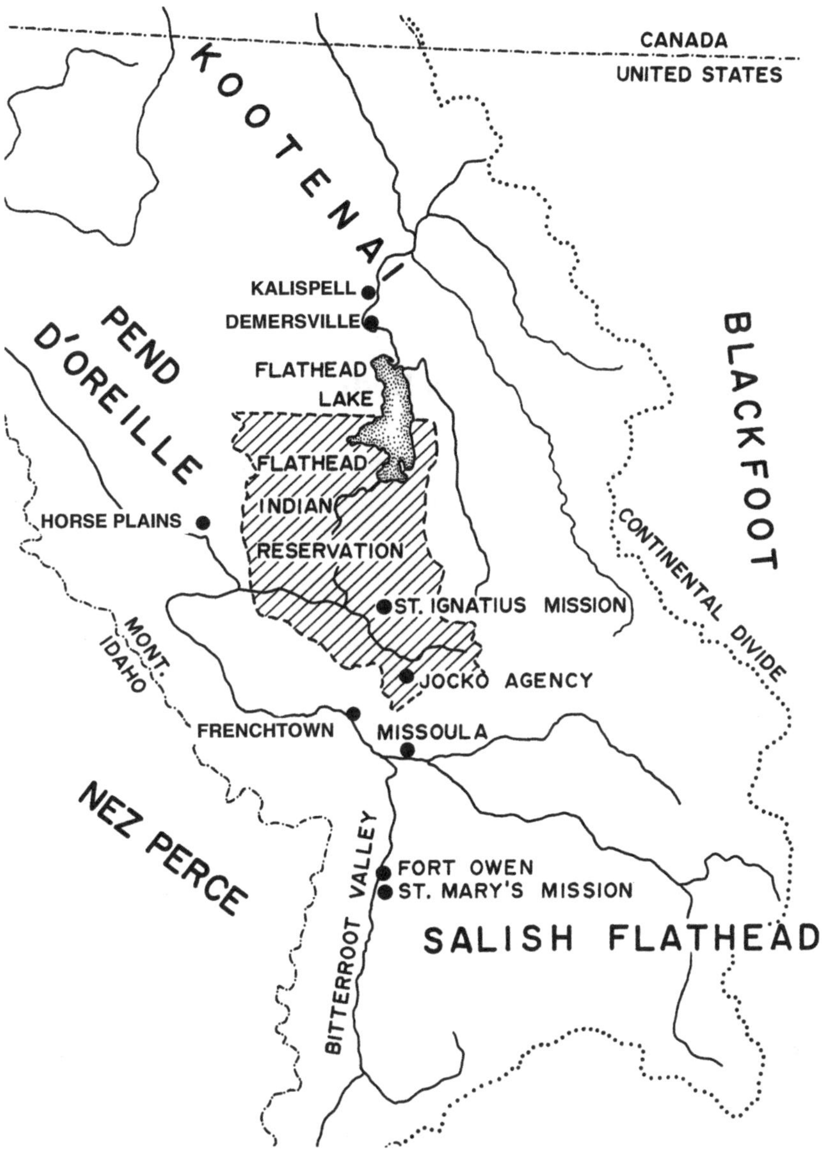

Flathead Indian Reservation
Showing Tribal Territories
and Surrounding Towns

Editor's Dedication

Dedicated to Cleo Kenmille, Kootenai lady nnd co-worker

Table of Contents

Editor's Preface

This book has been assembled from excerpts of the letters of Flathead Reservation Indian Agent Peter Ronan written to the U.S. Commissioner of Indian Affairs about Ronan's dealings with Eneas Big Knife, the chief of the Flathead Reservation Kootenai Indians between 1865 and 1900. The letters — from Ronan's first appointment as agent in 1877 to his death in 1893 — have been preserved in the National Archives in Washington, D.C. The correspondence describes Eneas' efforts to help his Kootenai Indian community adjust to the loss of the buffalo and other hunting resources in the late nineteenth century and to keep the peace with hostile white settlers in the Upper Flathead Valley.

Eneas used his government salary as chief to purchase agricultural equipment and tools to help the Kootenai expand their farms and horse and cattle herds. He struggled to get the biased white legal system to give justice to Kootenai Indians assaulted and murdered by white men. Eneas' own son, Sam, was murdered by a white man in Kalispell in 1891. In 1890 Eneas had been held hostage by the Missoula County Sheriff who was determined to punish Kootenai Indians accused of murdering white men while ignoring the crimes of white men who murdered Kootenai. Flathead Valley white men threatened open conflict to enable them to take Kootenai property and force the United States government to station army troops — and their spending — in the Flathead Valley.

Problems with the northern boundary of the Flathead Reservation forced Agent Ronan to issue off-reservation allotments just north of the reservation boundary to protect grazing and farm land long used by Kootenai ranchers and farmers. White men in the valley continually attacked and harassed the Kootenai, but Eneas relied on the weak protections the government provided for the Kootenai farmers. In December 1891, Agent Ronan actually succeeded in getting the Deputy U.S. Marshall to force most of the white trespassers off the Kootenai allotments. Unfortunately, the trespassers returned to harass the Kootenai land owners after the federal officials left the valley. After the death of Agent Ronan in 1893, later Flathead agents failed to continue his efforts to protect the Kootenai allotments.

Thanks to Eneas' wisdom and diplomacy, the Flathead Reservation Kootenai survived into the twentieth century. In his correspondence with the Commissioner of Indian Affairs, Agent Ronan expressed his respect for Chief Eneas and the role the chief played in late nineteenth century Montana history. The chief was a remarkable man.

Chief Eneas Bigknife
(1828-1900)
A Biographical Sketch

by Robert Bigart

Eneas, the chief of the Dayton Creek or Ksanka Kootenai for thirty-five years was born in 1828 to an Iroquois father, Big Knife, and a Kootenai mother, Suzette or Ahn-Akah.[1] The historical evidence suggested he was a remarkable man, and Flathead Indian Agent Peter Ronan obviously came to respect him highly over their years working together. During the 1880s and early 1890s, the reservation Kootenai faced white aggression in the Upper Flathead Valley, but somehow the Kootenai under Eneas' leadership were able to avoid war and continue the struggle to protect their interests and rights. The government often failed to fulfill its promises to protect Kootenai property and rights, but the small band avoided the destruction and death that could have resulted from open warfare.

As a young man, Eneas was a leading warrior and a war chief. He took part in repeated battles with the Blackfeet, Cree, and other tribes.[2] At six feet four inches tall, Eneas was an imposing figure.[3] According to Flathead Agent Charles Hutchins, Eneas became head chief on January 1, 1865, after his predecessor, Battiste, was killed by the Blackfeet while returning from the buffalo country. Eneas was only 37 years old then. In 1866, Flathead Agent Augustus Chapman requested funds to build a house for Eneas and his family.[4]

In his first annual report on August 13, 1877, Flathead Indian Agent Peter Ronan wrote that Eneas was "better respected and has more influence among his people than any other chief on the reservation." Ronan was especially impressed that Eneas used his salary as chief to purchase a mowing and reaping machine and a set of blacksmith's tools for the use of his tribe. Eneas was "a good man, kind and generous, and spends all the money he receives from Government in relieving the wants of his poor and struggling people."[5] In his August 12, 1879, report, Ronan commended Eneas for working to induce the Kootenai to turn to farming to replace the declining game and gathering resources in western Montana.[6] By 1879, the Kootenai had enclosed several farms.

By August 1885, Eneas and the Kootenai had 200 acres fenced and "about 1,000 bushels of wheat [were] raised in common, besides potatoes, turnips, cabbage, onions, carrots, parsnips, peas, &c."[7] But farming in common offended Ronan's Euro-American cultural values, and in August 15, 1886, Ronan proposed that a farmer be employed to show the Kootenai how to set up individual family farms like white people had.[8]

In 1883 when Joseph McCammon came to Montana to negotiate for the sale of the right-of-way for the Northern Pacific Railroad to cross the reservation, Eneas emphasized the importance of the reservation to the tribes. He questioned selling part of the reservation because: "It is a small country; it is valuable to us; we support ourselves by it; there is no end to these lands supporting us; they will do it for generations."[9]

Due to their location on the northern boundary of the reservation, the Kootenai were particularly affected by problems with the survey of the reservation boundary. Eneas and the Kootenai thought the northern line followed a ridge of hills which provided a well-defined natural boundary. The official survey placed the line several miles south of the natural boundary. In the twentieth century the U.S. Court of Claims decided the official boundary had been in error but still placed the line south of the boundary preferred by the Kootenai. This change in the northern boundary made it harder to keep white owned cattle off the reservation and also cut off hay and pasture land used for years by the Kootenai. Some of the white cattle owners paid Eneas for grazing, but trespassing cattle and loss of land caused problems for Eneas and his tribe for the rest of the nineteenth century.

During the late 1880s and early 1890s, the Kootenai continued to exercise their right to seasonally hunt, fish, and gather plants in the Upper Flathead Valley. Most of the Kootenai-white interactions were peaceful but some were complicated by language and cultural differences, alcohol, and white aggression. In 1888, two reservation Kootenai were lynched for murdering two white men at the head of Flathead Lake in 1887. After the lynching, an armed mob of white men invaded the reservation and confronted Eneas and the Kootenai. Eneas kept calm and was able to defuse the crisis and no further violence broke out. He did not object to the punishment of Kootenai murderers, but he felt they should at least receive a fair trial.[10]

In 1889, Eneas kept up his efforts to get justice while avoiding open warfare. Two white men killed a Kootenai Indian in an altercation that probably involved alcohol. Eneas threatened to kill the two guilty whites but made clear that other white people would not be harmed.[11]

In a June 8, 1889, council with Ronan and a special agent of the U.S. Justice Department about the whiskey problem, Eneas emphasized his work to punish Kootenai guilty of violence resulting from alcohol use. Traditional Kootenai practice had the chief use the whip to punish lawbreakers, but white officials opposed whipping because it offended nineteenth century white sensibilities. Eneas complained that without the whip, he could not control tribal members who got drunk and committed adultery or other crimes. He pointed out that the Kootenai did not have good jails, so he had no alternative punishment available. One account quotes Delima Demers Clifford, a tribal member, as seeing Eneas drinking alcohol on New Years Eve 1887. But, even if Eneas was not a teetotaler, he vigorously opposed the violence and other crimes that sometimes resulted from drinking.[12]

Eneas' struggle to get justice for the Kootenai while keeping the peace struck a personal note in August 1889 when his son, Samuel, was murdered by white people in Demersville. Eneas traveled to Demersville to find out what happened. The white people fed the Kootenai but refused to help bring the murderer to justice. The Demersville whites fumed and ranted that Eneas' visit had been an invasion. Ronan put Eneas' side of the story in writing, sent it to Washington, D.C., and had it published in a Helena newspaper and the Commissioner of Indian Affairs' annual report.[13] In December, Ronan tried to get the case before a grand jury, but the jury adjourned before he was able to get Eneas and the Indian witnesses to the courthouse. No one was ever punished for the murder.[14]

In July 1890, U.S. Army troops and a posse of white men surrounded the Kootenai camp and demanded that Eneas surrender Kootenai Indians accused of murdering white men. Eneas offered to cooperate, but he asked why white men who killed Kootenai were not also punished. According to newspaper reports, Missoula County Sheriff William Houston held Eneas hostage until the accused Indian murderers were surrendered, but Ronan's letters suggested Eneas decided himself to help the sheriff. Ronan wrote that Eneas did not object to Indian murderers being punished but wanted equal justice for white people who murdered Indians.[15] Father Jerome D'Aste, S.J., recorded the hostage version of Eneas' role in his diary.[16] One newspaper account noted that "it is largely due to his [Eneas'] aid that Pascale and other Indian criminals have been apprehended."[17] Two Kootenai Indians were convicted in a Montana court of murder and hung in Missoula in December 1890.

In January 1891, Robert H. Irvine, a mixed blood tribal member chosen by Eneas, was appointed as Kootenai farmer and moved to Dayton Creek to begin work. That October Eneas and the Kootenai brought several wagon-loads of wheat to the agency to be ground into flour. The trip of 60 miles to the agency took six days and a ferry crossing the Flathead River at the Foot of Flathead Lake. According to Ronan, Eneas was "much elated at the acchievement [sic]."[18]

That summer Eneas and the reservation Kootenai extended an invitation to the Bonners Ferry Kootenai to settle with them at Dayton Creek.[19]

In August 1891 Ronan traveled to the Kootenai camp and laid out off-reservation allotments for land just north of the official reservation boundary. The land had been used by the Kootenai for years believing it was on the reservation. Unfortunately, by December of that year, white homesteaders were already jumping the Kootenai allotments. Ronan was able to get the government to remove most of the first white trespassers, but others persisted in harassing the Kootenai farmers.[20]

In one particularly egregious example of white belligerence, Clarence Proctor actually built a fence around the improvements of a Kootenai farmer and claimed the right to the land in the enclosure, including the Kootenai farm.[21] In another case, Eugene McCarthy, a white settler who had worked on the erroneous boundary survey, claimed the land of a Kootenai farmer, Jean Jan Graw (Gingras), which contained a house, barn, and enclosed field that the Kootenai had occupied for twelve years. Eneas was crippled by rheumatism and hindered by language problems, but he tried to explain to McCarthy that the land belonged to the Kootenai farmer as a result of years of occupancy and a government allotment. McCarthy then proceeded to Demersville and filed charges against Eneas claiming that Eneas had personally threatened him. Ronan put up a bond for Eneas to appear in court on the charge since Eneas was too sick to travel just then. Apparently, the charges were later dropped as the case dragged on in the courts.[22] The restraint shown by Eneas and the aggrieved Kootenai farmers was remarkable. No open conflict flared, but white trespassers continued over the years to encroach on the Kootenai claims, and, after Ronan died in 1893, no one else remained to pressure the government to act. Finally in the early twentieth century the Kootenai had lost possession of almost all of the allotments and the government pressured the Kootenai allottees to relinquish their claims in return for small payments from the white trespassers.

On February 1, 1894, Eneas, most reservation tribal leaders, and many tribal members signed a petition asking for a resurvey of the northern boundary of the reservation, but then agent, Joseph Carter, panned it as a "matter worthy of little attention." The Commissioner of Indian Affairs refused to consider a resurvey.[23] In 1895 Eneas returned Goosta, a Kootenai Indian accused of horse stealing, to jail after he escaped.[24]

In much of the late 1890s, Eneas was confined to his bed and not able to exercise his authority as chief. Father Augustine Dimier, S.J., complained that Eneas' disability permitted gambling and other sins to infect Kootenai life.[25] Eneas died in 1900.[26]

Endnotes

1. "Kootenai Chiefs Memorial Draws Hundreds," *Char-Koosta* (Dixon, Mont.), vol. 2, no. 14 [Nov. 15, 1972], pp. 11-12; Chas. Hutchins to Montana Superintendent of Indian Affairs, June 30, 1865, U.S. Commissioner of Indian Affairs, *Annual Report of the Commissioner of Indian Affairs* (Washington, D.C.: U.S. Government Printing Office, 1865), p. 246; Harry Holbert Turney-High, *Ethnography of the Kutenai,* Memoir of the American Anthropological Association, No. 56 (1941), pp. 134-39; Carling Malouf and Thain White, "Kutenai Calendar Records," *Montana: Magazine of History*, vol. 3, no. 2 (Spring 1953), pp. 34-39.

2. Ronan letters, v. 2, pp. 42-45; Mary Ronan, *Frontier Woman: The Story of Mary Ronan as Told to Margaret Ronan,* ed. H. G. Merriam (Missoula: University of Montana Publications in History, 1973), pp. 124-25.

3. Rev. James O'Connor, "The Flathead Indians," *Records of the American Catholic Historical Society of Philadelphia*, vol. 3 (1888-1891), p. 104.

4. Chas. Hutchins to Montana Superintendent of Indian Affairs, June 30, 1865, U.S. Commissioner of Indian Affairs, *Annual Report of the Commissioner of Indian Affairs* (Washington, D.C.: U.S. Government Printing Office, 1865), p. 246; Augustus Chapman to CIA, Apr. 20,1866, U.S. Office of Indian Affairs, "Letters Received by the Office of Indian Affairs, 1824,-1880," National Archives Microfilm Publication M234, reel 488, fr. 178.

5. Ronan letters, vol. 1, pp. 20-24.

6. Ronan letters, vol. 1, pp. 111-14.

7. Ronan letters, vol. 1, pp. 316-21.

8. Ronan letters, vol. 1, pp. 360-64.

9. U.S. President, "Message from the President of the United States Transmitting a Letter from the Secretary of the Interior Respecting the Ratification of an Agreement with the Confederated Tribes of Flathead, Kootenay, and Upper Pend d'Oreilles Indians, for the Sale of a Portion of Their Reservation in Montana Territory," *Senate Executive Document* No. 44, 47th Congress, 2d Session (1883), serial 2076, p. 11.

10. Ronan letters, vol. 2, pp. 4-6.

11. Ronan letters, vol. 2, pp. 32-33.

12. Ronan letters, v. 2, pp. 42-45; E. D. Bannister to Secretary of Interior, Oct. 20, 1888, U.S. Department of the Interior, "Reports of Inspection of the Field Jurisdictions of the Office of Indian Affairs, 1873-1900," National Archives Microfilm Publication M1070, reel 11, Flathead Agency, 5261/1888, p. 6.

13. "The Red Man's Story," *Helena Journal* (daily), Oct. 25, 1889, p. 5, col. 1-2; Ronan letters, vol. 2, pp. 148-57.

14. Ronan letters, vol. 2, pp. 75-79, 80-83, 111-12, and 142-45.

15. Ronan letters, vol. 2, pp. 142, 142-45, 157-60, and 170-72.

16. Robert J. Bigart, ed., *Zealous in All Virtues: Documents of Worship and Culture Change, St. Ignatius Mission, Montana, 1890-1894* (Pablo, Mont.: Salish Kootenai College Press, 2007), p. 54.

17. "Four of a Kind," *Missoula Weekly Gazette*, Nov. 12, 1890, p. 3, col. 1-3.

18. Ronan letters, vol. 2, pp. 186-88, and 253-54.

19. Ronan letters, vol. 2, pp. 219-22.

20. Ronan letters, vol. 2, pp. 228 and 262-63.

21. Ronan letters, vol. 2, pp. 330-33.

22. Ronan letters, vol. 2, pp. 312, 313-16, and 330-33.

23. Joseph Carter to CIA, Feb. 6, 1894, 6,591/1894, NA CIA LR; CIA to Carter, Feb. 21, 1894, land, letterbook 274, pp. 394-96, NA CIA LS.

24. "Very Near a Good Indian," *The Kalispell Graphic*, Mar. 13, 1895, p. 3, col. 1.

25. Augustine Dimier to Rev. Father Provincial, Apr. 1901, Robert Bigart and Clarence Woodcock, eds., "St. Ignatius Mission, Montana: Reports from Two Jesuit Missionaries, 1885 & 1900-1901 (Part II)," *Arizona and the West,* vol. 23, no. 3 (Autumn 1981), pp. 275-76.

26. "Noted Chief Dead," *The Kalispell Bee,* July 27, 1900, p. 1, col. 5.

Chief Eneas Bigknife. Archives and Special Collections, Mansfield Library, University of Montana, Missoula, phto number 81-284

Chief Eneas Bigknife. *Tenth Annual Report of the Water Department, City of Kalispell, Montana* (Dec. 31, 1923), page 51.

The Ronan Letters

August 13, 1877

Excerpt from Peter Ronan to Commissioner of Indian Affairs, August 13, 1877, U.S. Commissioner of Indian Affairs, *Annual Report of the Commissioner of Indian Affairs* (Washington, D.C.: U.S. Government Printing Office, 1877), pp. 530-533.

The Kootenais.

.... This year six families of that tribe have entered upon civilizing pursuits and have excellent crops of wheat, oats, potatoes, onions, turnips, &c. The tribe also owns 100 head of horned stock and 300 head of horses. These poor people, above all others on this reservation, need encouragement and assistance, as they are furnished with hardly any implements of labor worth speaking of. A few weeks ago Eneas, the Kootenai chief, who, by the way, is better respected and has more influence among his people than any other chief on the reservation, purchased for the use of his tribe a mowing and reaping machine and a set of blacksmith's tools, pledging in payment the money coming to him from Government for the next two quarters as chief of the tribe. Eneas is a good man, kind and generous, and spends all the money he receives from Government in relieving the wants of his poor and struggling people.

The Kootenais live near the Flathead Lake, nearly 100 miles from the agency, and have no means of hauling lumber from the agency mill, and therefore have no houses to live in. If means are given these people to continue their efforts and encourage their civilizing pursuits, under the chieftainship of Eneas, whom the whole tribe respect and venerate, a very short time will elapse before they become a happy and prosperous people, as their land is productive and their grazing facilities unsurpassed. I would therefore recommend that the case of the Kootenais be carefully considered and prompt action be taken in furnishing them with implements of labor.

August 12, 1878

Excerpt from Peter Ronan to Commissioner of Indian Affairs, August 12, 1878, U.S. Commissioner of Indian Affairs, *Annual Report of the Commissioner of Indian Affairs* (Washington, D.C.: U.S. Government Printing Office, 1878), pp. 87-89.

> Editor's note: Ronan mentions Chief Eneas' use of personal funds to encourage farming among the Kootenai. The collapse

of the buffalo herds and other game resources undermined the ability of the Kootenai and other tribes to support themselves through traditional hunting and gathering.

Building.

This year some good, substantial houses have been erected by the Indians, and lumber and shingles from the mill have been in great demand. The Indians cut and haul their own logs to the mill, and the agency miller saws them into lumber to suit their convenience. Several more houses would have been erected by the Kootenays but for the fact that the mill is some 60 miles distant from their village, and there are but three wagons in the tribe with which to do their hauling and farming. The chief of the Kootenays is doing all in his power to induce his people to follow the thrifty habits of the generality of the Flatheads and Pend d'Oreilles, and from his own private means has purchased for the use of his tribe a combined mowing and reaping machine, a set of carpenter tools, also, a set of blacksmith tools. I would again urge the necessity of encouraging these people by assisting them with agricultural implements, wagons, and harness, as well as the needy of the other two tribes.

August 1885

Excerpt from Peter Ronan to Commissioner of Indian Affairs, August 1885, U.S. Commissioner of Indian Affairs, *Annual Report of the Commissioner of Indian Affairs* (Washington, D.C.: U.S. Government Printing Office, 1885), pp. 126-129.

Dayton Creek. — Eneas, chief of the Kootenais, 200 acres fenced for use of tribe, about 1,000 bushels of wheat raised in common, besides potatoes, turnips, cabbage, onions, parsnips, peas, &c [in 1885].

April 17, 1888

LR 10,741/1888, RG 75, National Archives, Washington, D.C.

Editor's note: The 1887 murder of two white prospectors on Wolf Creek and the 1888 lynching of the Flathead Reservation Kootenai accused of the crime introduced a troubled period of Kootenai-white relations in the Upper Flathead Valley. Ralph Ramsdell was one of the leaders of the white vigilantes who lynched the suspected murderers. In the face of the hostile provocations by Ramsdell and the white posse, Chief Eneas' restraint and adroit diplomacy in avoiding open hostilities was remarkable. Eneas obviously disapproved of the murder of the white miners, but he and Ronan objected to lynch justice. Ramsdell's racist version of the lynching and confrontation with Eneas was published in "Horrible Massacre," *The Weekly Missoulian.*[1]

United States Indian Service,
Flathead Agency,
April 17th, 1888.

Hon. Commissioner of Indian Affairs
Washington, D.C.

Sir:

Herewith I have the honor to forward copy of report which I mad[e] at the request of Brigadier Gen. Thos N. Ruger, and which will explain itself.

I have the honor to be
Your obedient servant
Peter Ronan
United States Indian Agt.

Enclosure:

United States Indian Service
Flathead Agency, M.T.
April 17th, 1888.

Thos. H. Ruger
Brigadier General,
Commanding Department of Dakota,
St. Paul, Minn.

Sir:

In reply to your letter of April 12th, 1888, calling attention to the newspaper reports of trouble about Ashley, at the Head of the Flathead Lake, and asking for such information as I may be able to furnish, I would respectfully state that it is a fact that the citizens of that vicinity did execute two Kootenai Indians some time last month, and that a third one made his escape or he would also follow the fate of the other two.

From diligent inquiries among the Indians of this reservation, I am afraid that the reported murder of the whitemen is true, and that no mistake was made by the citizens as to the identity of the Indian murderers. As near as I can ascertain the whitemen were Killed about the 17th of last June, at a place called Woolf [sic] Creek beyond Pleasant Valley, on the trail leading to Horse Plains. The Indians who committed the crime, and who were lynched, are said to belong to the band of Chief Eneas, who have their homes on this reservation, and live about sixty miles north of the Agency, at Dayton Creek. One of the murderers, who is still at large, confessed the crime to reliable Indians of this reserve, who gave the information, which I give to you as furnished to me: It seems that a party of some ten Kootenai Indians while passing along the trail noticed three whitemen encamped and cooking their meal. One Indian proposed to two others to go to the camp and intimidate the whites. On nearing them the Indians fired over their heads; but the whitemen only laughed at it as a joke, whereupon one of the Indians proposed to kill them and the others agreed. Two of the white party being seated eating, in range, a bullet fired by an Indian passed through both men Killing them instantly. The third was fired upon and wounded and was killed by the blows of an axe or hatchet. No motive was given for the crime when the story was told of the bloody work.

I sent for Chief Eneas, of the reservation Kootenais, and he stated in the interview that while on his way to St. Ignatius Mission, a few days before Easter Sunday, he was overtaken by an Indian who informed him that a party of armed whitemen, from the Head of the Lake, were at Dayton Creek looking for him. The chief stated that he turned back and met the whitemen and asked why they were there searching for him with arms. The leader of the whites talked the Kootenai language — his name is Ramsdale, and last summer he Kept a trading post near the British line, some six miles south on the American side. This man replied that they had hung two of his Indians and were there to find out what he was going to do about it. It was explained to Eneas, that a white traveller [sic] who camped near Dayton Creek, on hearing of the hanging of the Indians, mounted a horse and rode into Ashley, and stated that the band of Eneas were in Arms — that they had attacked him and he made his escape while the Indians were plundering his wagon. This was easily refuted by Eneas, who told the whites that the wagon was standing where the man encamped; that no Indian molested him or his property, and it was easy to ascertain that fact by examination, which was made by the whites and nothing was found disturbed. The action of the whiteman who caused the excitement on the reservation is inexcusable and might have caused a fight but for the fact that the matter was so quickly and satisfactorily explained on both sides.

Chief Eneas in his statement to me, while he was reticent in regard to having heard of any confession from his people in regard to the murder, stated that if murder had been committed by the Indians it was nothing more than justice to hang the guilty ones; but was sorry that the Lake settlers took the law into their own hands and lynched the prisoners, as a trial, conviction and execution by due process of law would have a more salutory effect upon the Indians and prevent recourse to revenge.

In regard to the state of things relative to security of the white settlers in the region north of the Flathead Lake, I think there is no cause to fear. To my knowledge there has been no change since last year, and the handful of North Kootenai Indians south of the border, in the Tobacco Plains region have not increased since last Summer and fall and have no such idea of making war on the whites.

As it appears the Indians who were lynched did not belong to the Tobacco Plains band, but to that of Chief Eneas, of this reservation, I repeat I cannot see what cause the settlers can have for excitement, especially as the Chief of the band to which the culprits belonged states that no trouble will come from him or his people, as it is a conceded fact they were unjustifiable murderers of whitemen and deserved their fate whether by lynch law or otherwise.

The suppression of the sale of whisky to Indians on the border would prevent lawlessness and the settlers should make an effort to that end.

I hope for the establishment of a military post in that region has a great tendency, I think, to Keep up excitement and to Exagerate [sic] the real state of affairs.

I am, very respectfully,
Your ob'd't servant,
[blank]
United States Indian Agent.

March 4, 1889

LR 5,921/1889, telegram, RG 75, National Archives, Washington, D.C.

> Editor's note: Chief Eneas' threat of revenge referred to by Ronan seemed to have been an example of Eneas' efforts to avoid general conflict with the whites while still seeking justice for his people.

3/4, 1889
Flat Head Agency Arlee Mont

To Indian Commissioner,
Washn D.C.

News reached me that an indian who was struck on the head with a revolver by one J. E. Clifford at head of Flathead Lake has since died from wound. It is stated that Chief Eneas and the father of the victim say that while they will not trouble innocent people they will Kill Clifford at all hazards. I start at once to Allay excitement among indians & to have arrests made.

Ronald [sic], Agent.

June 12, 1889

LR 16,035/1889, RG 75, National Archives, Washington, D.C.

> Editor's note: This account of a June 8, 1889, council with Ronan, Special Agent of the Department of Justice H. M. Marchant, Chief Eneas, and Chief Michelle of the Pend d'Oreille emphasized Eneas' efforts to maintain peace with the white settlers in the Upper Flathead Valley. In 1888 a mob of white men had lynched two Kootenai Indians accused of murder and then surrounded the Kootenai camp at Dayton and threatened Eneas. Eneas kept calm and defused the situation so it did not lead to more bloodshed. As he said in this council, he worked hard to keep his young men out of trouble, but local whites sold them whiskey. While Eneas asked for justice and government support to keep the peace, Marchant was primarily worried about the use of whipping for punishment. Since public whippings offended late nineteenth century white sensibilities, the Commissioner of Indian Affairs ordered them stopped. Without whippings to punish misbehavior, the reservation needed a new jail.[2]

United States Indian Service,
Flathead Agency,
June 12, 1889.

Hon. Commissioner of Indian Affairs
Washington, D.C.

Sir:

In compliance with the request of Captain Henry M. Marchant, Special Agent of the Department of Justice, I accompanied that gentleman to the Foot of Flathead Lake, on this reservation, where I called an Indian Council, for the purpose of obtaining Indian evidence against whisky trading whitemen, who make a business of selling whisky to Indians. Also to inquire into and get evidence against a mob of white men who took the law into their own hands and hung two Kootenai Indians of this reservation, and who after the hanging, with arms in their hands, surrounded the camp of Chief Eaneas, on this reservation, for the purpose of intimidation etc.

On the 8th of June the Indian Council met, and I herewith have the honor to submit a synopsis of the proceedings:

After the usual hand shaking and greeting were over Agent Ronan addressed his interpreter:

Tell Chief Eneas I agreed to meet him and his head men here two weeks ago, but one of his men was killed at the Head of the Lake, and I followed and captured the murderer at Great Falls, on the Missouri river, and that is the reason I did not get here on time.

Now tell Eneas that I have very little to say — only what I am here for and what Captain Marchant is here for. Tell him that for the last two years the drunkeness has been much worse then at any time since I came here — twelve years ago; also the debauchery of women by the young men of the tribes. It is my opinion that the beginning of all Indian trouble is whisky. When whisky comes on the reserve then commences all other crimes. I have asked from Washington the Great Fathers assistance to put a stop to this whisky selling to Indians. The Great Father ordered the Judge or Chief Justice to send some one here to put a stop to it, and he has sent this gentleman, Captain Henry M. Marchant, Special Agent from the Department of Justice, at Washington, to assist me in this effort to suppress the sale of whisky to the Indians.

Now tell Eneas, that something over a year ago two of his people were hung by a mob at the Head of the Lake; that though the Indians may have been guilty, no mob had a right to hang them. That is what the law is for — to punish crime; that is why taxes are paid — why we have Judges, Courts, Sheriffs and jails — why we have law! In the eyes of the law a croud [sic] of men who take a man and hang him are looked upon as criminals. It is the duty of Eneas or any of his men present, if they know the names of any of the men who did this hanging to give their names to Captain Marchant. It is also the duty of Chief Eneas and his men, and also of the Pend 'd Oreille Chief Michel, who is present, and his men, if they know, to give the names of any white men who are or have been guilty of selling whisky to Indians. If any present have bought whisky, it is their duty to give names, time and place to Captain Marchant.

Now I have only to add that there is a big steer in the corrall, and some sugar, coffee, flour etc., at my camp, and to send men after them and others to butcher the beef, and while the women are preparing the feast, Captain Marchant, through my interpreter will talk with Eaneas and Michel, and he and Mr. [Henry] Lambert will take what evidence they may have to present.

Captain Marchant to the Interpreter:

Say to Eneas that the Agent, Major Ronan has fully explained to them my mission here. I came from Washington to put a stop to selling whisky to Indians by whitemen, and that I need their assistance, and without it it will be almost impossible for me to do it; but if they will give me their aid I will do my utmost to stop it. I am here for their good and if they will put confidence in me I will help them. Important business calls the Major back to the Agency. I shall go to the Head of the Lake and make investigation as to who is selling whisky to Indians, and other matters connected with the good of the Indians. Say to Eneas that I want to ask him a few questions now.

Chief Eneas: Before answering you I desire to say a few words:

Michel [Revais, the interpreter], tell the Agent when the Great Father first sent him to us, he was a much younger man than he is to-day. His children have grown up around him on our reservation and I see one of his boys with him who was born in our country.

I was also young and strong — I looked like a Chief — I felt like a Chief. In my youth our Nation was at war with a great many tribes, and the last of our enemies that we made peace with were the Blackfeet. I was the War Chief of my tribe and was called Big Knife. To-day we are at peace with all of our enemies. The Blackfeet are our friends, and some of their children are at school with our children at the Mission. Until within a few years, there were few white people near our reservation. Now they surround us on all sides, thick almost as the leaves of the forest. When you came here there was only one white family living at Horse Plains. No white people at all at Thompson Falls; no miners in the Coer'd Alenes; and where the big city of Spokane Falls now stands I remember of but two white families living there. At the Head of the Flathead Lake where you are now going there was but one or two white men and no white families. Missoula had a small settlement of whites, but now it is a great big town — full of white people. In the days I speak of my young men could get but very little whisky — none knew the taste of it but those who hung around your settlement. It is different to-day! They have acquired the habit and love the influence of whisky, and in spite of your laws can procure all they can pay for. In old times I would take my whip in my hand and chastise any of my Indians that broke the law either by getting drunk or committing audultry [sic] or any other crime, and they feared me and my authority the same as your children fear your authority and chastisement as a father when they do wrong. I could controll my children then — I call all my tribe my children. Take the whip from my hand I have no controll. We have no good jails like the white people — no other mode of punishment in our camp, and the wild and desolute young men laugh at talk when it is not followed by punishment. The heart of a white man must be very small if he cannot see the necessity of authority by a chief in an Indian camp; and when I loose the use of the whip I loose all power to controll my people. I hope the Chief who has come here from Washington will help us. I am now ready to answer his questions.

Here the investigation and taking of evidence commenced, which I trust will soon lead to the arrest of guilty parties.

In reference to the remarks of Eneas about the use of the whip among the Indians, for the punishment of certain transgressions I would respectfully state that it has always been the rule of the tribes to use it. Captain Marchant made some objection to this as one of their modes of punishment; when the Judges and the policemen notified me that they would resign if they could not continue their own methods of punishment for crime. They claimed, with truth, that they had no good jail, and no other punishment to substitute that would strike terror where young men were guilty of drunkeness, running off with the wives of industrious Indians, debauching young girls of the tribes etc., etc. They also claim that they use the whip with moderation and practice no cruelty, and that the mere disgrace of being publicly flogged, however lightly, has more effect in keeping the young people straight than any other mode of punishment. I must say that I know of no act of cruelty practiced by the Indian Chiefs, Judges or Policemen, and all stories to that effect are mere exagerations. I have promised the Indians to submit the matter to the Hon. Commissioner of Indian Affairs, and if, after Captain Marchants report is received, by his Department, he decides to order the abolishment of the whip altogether I shall so notify the Indians.

I herewith have the honor to enclose vouchers for expenses incurred in calling and feeding the Indians during the council, and have the honor to be

Your obedient servant
Peter Ronan
United States Indian Agent.

September 1, 1889

LR 25,223/1889, RG 75, National Archives, Washington, D.C. The attached clippings referred to in the letter were sent to D.C. on September 6 and are filed under 25,629/1889.

> Editor's note: The alcohol saturated conflict in Demersville in late August 1889 resulted in the death of Kootenai Chief Eneas' son, Sam. Many versions of the events were recorded by white participants and witnesses over the years, so it was hard to sort out the facts. Chief Eneas' account in Ronan's September 9, 1889, letter, below, seems reasonable. The Ramsdell brothers, who served as both whiskey dealers and law officers, had already been in conflict with Ronan in the past.[3] The trouble was widely reported across the country.[4] The Commissioner of Indian Affairs immediately telegraphed Ronan to investigate.[5] See Ronan's September 9, 1889, letter for Chief Eneas' remarkable restraint in the affair.

United States Indian Service,
Flathead Agency,
September 1st, 1889.

Hon. Commissioner Indian Affairs
Washington, D.C.

Sir:

I have the honor to submit my report for the month of August and in doing so sincerely regret to be compelled to notice the exaggerated press reports, and also the fanaticism and prejudice which is being inculcated by persons who have an interest to the prejudice of the Indians and the breaking up of their reservation could the same be accomplished by fair means or foul.

I herewith enclose copy of resolutions passed by some citizens at the Head of Flathead Lake, and submit my explanations.[6] U.S. Inspector Junkin is now upon the reservation, and I believe that after an investigation, that his report if noticed will bear me out in its details. The Chairman W. R. Ramsdell has figured before in my communications to your office, as a suspected Indian whisky trader, but now a full fledged politician for Legislative honors in the Democratic ticket in Montana.

To illustrate the character of this man, I beg to submit copy of a letter I wrote to the Indian Commissioner of British Columbia in answer to inquiries about this same individual.

Flathead Agency, Montana Ter.
February 2nd, 1887

I. W. Powell
Indian Commissioner Victoria
British Columbia

Sir:

I am in receipt of your letter of January 14th 1887, and in reply thereto would state that the store or trading post of Ramsdell Brothers, on Tobacco Plains, is in the neighborhood of one hundred miles north of the Boundary Line of this Indian reservation, and embraced in the County of Missoula, Territory of Montana. You complain that the above named firm are in the habit of selling liquors in quantities, and that many of the natives of that place have lately been intoxicated. I should be glad to put a stop to the traf[f]ic referred to if in my power, but I can only refer the matter to the authorities of Missoula County, and to the United States Marshal of Montana Territory.

As the store of Ramsdell Brothers is in the neighborhood of only about six miles from the British Border, if your information is correct in regard to the sale of intoxicating liquors to the natives, no doubt it affords an opportunity for the Indians of either side of the line to indulge in their habits of intoxication and should be looked after by the proper authorities, the trafic broken up and offenders punished.

I am respectfully your obedient ser'vt
(Signed) Peter Ronan
U.S. Ind. Agt.

Replying to a letter from W. H. Ruger, Brigadier General, Commanding the Department of Dakota, under date of April 17th, 1888 — his letter being dated April 12th of same month, in which he called attention of newspaper reports of trouble at the Head of Flathead Lake, and asking for such information as I might be able to furnish. I stated it was a fact that the citizens of that vicinity did unlawfully execute two Kootenai Indians, some time in the month of March of that year, and that a third one made his escape or he would follow the fate of the others. Leaving out the details as to the supposed murder of whitemen by the Indians who were unlawfully hung I wrote to the General that I sent for Chief Eneas, of the reservation Kootenais, and that he stated in the interview that while on his way to St. Ignatius Mission a few days before Easter Sunday, he was overtaken by an Indian who informed him that a party of armed whitemen from the Head of the Lake were on the reservation at Dayton Creek, looking for him. The Chief stated that he turned back and met the whitemen and asked by what authority they wer[e] on the reservation searching for him with arms.

The leader of the whites whose name was W. R. Ramsdell the same person who figures in the complaint of Major Powell talked the Kootenai language, and the summer before kept a trading post and whisky shop near the British line, some six miles south on the American side. This man Ramsdell replied (said the Chief) that he was the authority and they had hung two of his Indians and were there to find out what he was going to do about it. The action of Ramsdell and party for coming on the reservation in arms was inexcusable, and might have caused great bloodshed, but for the forbearance of the Indian Chief. Eneas stated to me that if murder had been committed by the Indians it was nothing more than justice to hang the guilty ones but was sorry that Ramsdell and party took the law into their own hands and lynched the Indians, as their trial and conviction and execution by due process of law would have a better effect upon the Indians and prevent recourse to revenge. Continuing this matter, I would respectfully refer the Hon. Commissioner of Indian Affairs to my monthly report dated March 1st 1889, and would take the liberty to here copy an extract which bears upon the history of the feeling existing between the Kootenai Indians, and the settlers at the Head of Flathead Lake.

"Considerable excitement prevailed throughout Montana recently and exagerated reports were telegraphed to the Associated press of a probably Indian uprising on this reservation. The rumored trouble grew out of the fact that one J. E. Clifford, who keeps a store in Demersville at the Head of the Flathead Lake, and North of the reservation, beat an Indian over the head with a pistol. It was first reported that the Indians in revenge killed Clifford, and a Doctor Cuningham. This was false. The Chief of the Kootenai tribe to whom the assaulted Indian belonged stated that while he could not blame the settlers at the Head of Flathead Lake, who were innocent of the doing of one or two men, that if the wounded Indian died Clifford would be killed at all hazzards. The Indian died. I procured the arrest of Clifford and Dr. Cuningham as accessory and had them brought to the town of Missoula. The case was examined, but the Grand jury failed to find indictments much to the disappointment of the Indians, who claimed that Clifford should at least be indicted and tried in open court, as they believe him to have committed an unjustifiable crime."

I now beg to refer the Hon. Commissioner to my report dated June 12th, 1889, in which I stated that Captain Henry M. Marchant Special Agent from the Department of Justice, was then on the reservation and I accompanied him to the Flathead Lake, and called an Indian Council for the purpose of obtaining Indian evidence against whisky trading whitemen, who make a business of selling whisky to Indians at the head of Flathead Lake, also to try to get evidence against a mob of whitemen who hung two Kootenai Indians at the same place taking the law into their own hands, thus imperiling the lives of innocent parties from revengeful feelings of the Indians, who saw two of their people taken from the hands of a deputy sheriff by a lawless mob and hung in handcuffs, without trial or investigation.

To add to all of this two weeks ago, the enclosed exciting press reports were furnished. Upon investigation on the reservation, and without going to Demersville something like one hundred miles from here, which requires travel by team or horseback, and also by steamboat, I found that the sale of whisky to the Indians was the cause of the trouble, and that the Indians admitted that one Indian had killed another, who was his brotherinlaw, and that no trouble would follow as the whites were not considered blameble. The Indian killed was the son of the Chief of the Kootenai tribe, and without my knowledge, he took some of his men to the scene of the murder, and claims without any hostile intent, but to ascertain for himself whether his son was killed by the whites or by his own soninlaw. If by whites, he would demand the arrest and punishment of the murderer of his son — and also stated that as the settlers hung two of his people for a murder, he thought it was no more than just that the slayer of his son if a whiteman should be tried and punished by whitemen. He also claimed that he wished to implore the white people not to sell whisky to the Indians, as that was the cause of all the unfriendeliness [sic] between the Indians and the settlers.

This visit of Chief Eneas to Demersville has been exagerated, and the resolutions published, I believe to excite public opinion against the investigation of the hanging of the Kootenai Indians by the next Grand Jury, also investigations into the sale of whisky to the Indians in that settlement, and to injure the influence and standing of your humble servant. In my last I reported the hay crop almost a total failure, and also that the grain and vegetable crop has suffered in the same way, and that not a quarter of the usual amount can be harvested this year.

I took accasion to cut several tons of coarse wild rye grass, which I had stacked. While not fit for horses, if the winter is hard it will do very well for the Indians to feed to cattle. Last week I sent the threshing machine out and the light crops are being threshed by the Indians. The sawmill has been in operation for the past week cutting lumber from logs delivered by Indians to be used by them in erecting shed and houses this fall.

All interests pertaining to the well fare of the Indians are in good shape, and I have the honor herewith to inclose sanitary report and report of funds and indebtedness for the month of August and also report of farmer, and am

Very respectfully your obedient servant
Peter Ronan
United States Indian Agent.

September 9, 1889

LR 26,690/1889, RG 75, National Archives, Washington, D.C.

> Editor's note: The killing of Chief Eneas' son, Samuel, in Demersville was a tragic affair and the historical records include many contradictory sources. The local whites seemed to be very anxious to blame an Indian for the killing, but this was possibly a self-serving falsehood.[7] Eneas' statement emphasized his diplomatic efforts to protect his tribe while also avoiding further bloodshed. He controlled his anger, despite the provocations from many of the Upper Flathead Valley whites. Ronan had Eneas' side of the story published in a Helena newspaper and his 1890 annual report to the Commissioner of Indian Affairs.[8] In response to this report, the Commissioner of Indian Affairs decided the killing may have been "totally without justification" and asked the Secretary of the Interior to have the United States Attorney for Montana investigate.[9] He also instructed Ronan to cooperate in the investigation.[10] The Commissioner

of Indian Affairs then received various communications from white officials blaming the Indians for the conflict and asking for protection from the Kootenai. He requested that the U.S. Army investigate the conflicting claims.[11] A grand jury was convened but there was no record of anyone being punished for Sam's death.[12] The reminiscences of Claude R. Gregg, a white Kalispell resident, stated that his grandfather shot Sam and then the Demersville whites tried to blame a white vagrant who fled the area.[13] See also Ronan's letters of October 22, 1889, and November 29, 1889.[14] A similar case of a Kootenai being shot in an alley made the newspapers in 1896. In that case Susan Kiona was murdered in a Kalispell alley, but no one was ever convicted.[15]

To add to the tension, in August 1889 someone burned haystacks at Dayton belonging to Gravelle, LeBeau, and Chief Eneas.[16]

United States Indian Service,
Flathead Agency,
September 9th, 1889.

Hon. Commissioner of Indian Affairs
Washington, D.C.

Sir:

With the hope of bringing certain criminals to justice, that live in the settlements at the Head of the Flathead Lake, I shall go to the County Seat of Missoula County, where the Grand Jury is now in session, and bring before them the following statement made to me by Eneas, Chief of the Kootenai Indians of this reservation. It refers to the events and cause of the last sensational reports published through the country of an Indian uprising in that region, and is as follows:

Chief Eneas:

Three Indian boys of my band were gambling near Oust Finley's place on Mud Creek on the reservation. They lost everything they had even to their blankets. They then started for the Head of the Lake going up the East side, and avoiding my home which is on the West side. On the way they passed a creek where there are some white settlers, about one mile from Demersville. At that place a whiteman who was on foot took a horse away from another whiteman who was riding the same. The fellow who was set afoot begged of the Indians to loan him a horse to ride home, which they did and turned back with him. The Man's name is Joe Morant and he is a settler at the Head of the Lake. He gave the Indian boys whisky upon which they got drunk. When they got to Demersville they were drunk from the whisky obtained from Morant. At Demersville, they got into trouble and a whiteman drew a pistol on one of them but a fight was prevented by outsiders. I (Eneas) was camped near Chief Michel's place, and the day after the Indian boys mentioned started for Demersville, I moved my camp to go home. I camped for the night near the Steamboat landing at the Foot of the Lake. My son-in-law, Louie having loaned a horse to the Indian boys he took the steamer to Demersville to get him back. Before getting on the steamer Louie asked my son to take his horse and ride up to Demersville and meet him there. When I got to my home at Dayton Creek, my son and another Indian rode to Demersvill[e]. They had no arms when they left. They camped the first night with some Pend 'd Oreilles and Kootenais on this side of Demersville. In the morning they found the three Indian boys, the party altogether being six Indians. They sat around the store all day at Demersville. In the evening, two of the boys who previously got whisky from Morant were approached by a whiteman who came out of a saloon, and who is known to the Indians by the name of Jack Sheppard. He asked the boys if they wanted to buy whisky. The Indian boys replied that they had no money; they then reported to their companions that a whiteman offered to sell them whisky. My son-in-law Louie had money and he gave the boys four dollars to buy with. They found Jack and gave him the money. Jack pointed out a place on the bank of the river where he would deliver the whisky. True to agreement Jack returned with two bottles of whisky, which they carried to the other Indians. They all went away from the vicinity of the store to a more secluded spot and commenced drinking. One bottle was drank by six Indians, and my son after drinking said he was hungry and started to the hotel to get something to eat. My son in law Louie followed him. Louie heard a white man talking loud to my son through an upstairs window, ordering him to go away or he would shoot him. Lou[i]e took my son by the arm and tried to take him away. Louie said he heard some one come down stairs who came out the door and while he (Louie) held my son the white man shot him. When my son fell, Louie stated that the man who shot him told him to get away quick or he would be shot. Lou[i]e could not run as he is lame but he turned and saw two white men with guns who told him to get away, and followed him as he hobbled off, for about a hundred yards. Two of the Indian boys who got the whisky started that night after the shooting, for Tobacco Plains, and the other three Indians started back to my home on the reservation. They told me that white men killed my son at Demersville. I sent a whiteman called "Savia" [Francois Gravelle] who is married to a Kootenai woman to get the body of my son. When "Savia" returned with the dead body he told me that the white people at Demersville wanted me to go up there. The morning after the Killing a camp of British Kootenais arrived at Demersville from Tobacco Plains, and they recognized the body as being that of my son. The whitemen told them also to tell me to come to Demersville. I did not wish to go but was advised by a white man who lives in the Lake country to go. It was sixty miles from my home to the Agency and I started for Demersville without letting you (the Agent) know as the distance was so far. I took some of my people along, but sent word ahead that I was coming with no hostile intent, but simply to inquire if my son was killed by whitemen or not. If so to ask that the murder might be punished, and the men who sold the whisky might also be punished, as that was all the cause of the trouble between my Indians and whitemen. I camped on the night of my arrival at the house of Baptist Le Bow [J. B. LeBeau], who is a white settler and lives on this side of Demersville. In the morning I sent another man to let the people know I was coming to talk with them as a friend. When I got to Demersville the people seemed excited and afraid that I came there for revenge. I assured them through an interpreter as best I could my friendly intentions. I could not get any good council with them. I knew that not one of my Indians who had the trouble had a gun or a pistol with them when they left my camp for the Head of the Lake. I do not know where any of them could have borrowed or purchased a pistol or a gun. I told the people if they could tell me where any one of them got a gun or pistol then I might think my son was killed by an Indian. One of the Indians sold a horse to a white man. I asked that white man if he traded a gun or a pistol for the horse — he said no! I asked to see the ball which killed my son, and was answered that the ball was sent to the Agent (not so it was no[t] sent) and by him it would [be] sent to Missoula. Louie, my son-in-law told the whites at Demersville, in answer to a question that he saw the gun plainly in the hands of a white man which killed my son — that it was not a pistol but a gun which looked like a Winchester. Louie also claimed that he could recognize the man who held the gun, and was asked to do so if he was present. Louie pointed out the man but he was not arrested. That man lives in a house at Demersville, but Louie does not know his name, but can point out the house. Finding that I could not learn anything about who killed my son; whether it was a white man as claimed by the Indians; or by an Indian as claimed by the whitemen. I came home to my place at Dayton Creek. The whites wished me to stay one day longer but I felt it would be useless to do so.

I now leave it in the hands of the white men for investigation, and I trust they will do me the justice to investigate this killing. My Indians claim it was done by whitemen, the white men claim it was done by Indians. God Knows! I do not. I now throw myself upon your sense of justice to all.

A great many of my people have been killed by white men; two of them were hung by a mob. I know of no punishment or even a trial that was ever given to a white man for killing any of my Indians, and I now think it time to show that there is justice to be accorded to the Indians as well as to the whites. If this matter shall be brought before the Court at Missoula I am ready to be there and also to do all in my power to bring in witnesses who might be required.

Eneas Chief of Kootenais
his X mark

Respectfully submitted
Peter Ronan, U.S. Indian Agent.

October 22, 1889

LR 30,609/1889, RG 75, National Archives, Washington, D.C.

> Editor's note: See annotation for Ronan's September 9, 1889, letter for more information about the murder of Chief Eneas' son, Samuel.
>
> General Henry B. Carrington came to the Bitterroot Valley to negotiate the sale of the Bitterroot Salish allotments following the failure of their crops during the 1889 drought. Carrington was able to convince Charlo to remove, but he made commitments the government did not honor. He left a legacy of bitterness and broken promises. The two-year delay in the removal until 1891 further impoverished the Bitterroot Salish. They relied on Carrington's word that the removal would take place during spring 1890 and did not plant crops during 1890 or 1891.

United States Indian Service,
Flathead Agency, Mont.
October 22d, 1889.

The Hon. Commissioner of Indian Affairs
Washington, D.C.

Sir:

In replying to your letter dated October 14th, 1889, "L28659 – 1889" referring to my communication dated September 9th, 1889, submitting the statement of Eneas, Chief of the Kootenai Indians, relative to the killing of his son at Demersville, in this Territory, I have to say that I am also, in receipt of a letter from E. D. Weed, United States Attorney for Montana, upon this subject and I have the honor herewith to enclose copy of my reply to that officer, which will explain the situation to you.

I am, very respectfully,
Your obedient servant,
Peter Ronan
U.S. Indian Agent.

Enclosure:

(Copy)

United States Indian Service,
Flathead Agency, Montana
October 22d, 1889.

E. D. Weed, Esq.,
U.S. Attorney for Montana,
Helena, M.T.

Dear Sir:

I am in receipt of your favor of the 16th inst., with the information that you received a communication from the Attorney General, with enclosures from the Secretary of the Interior and the Commissioner of Indian Affairs, relating to the Killing of the son of Chief Eneas, of the Kootenai Indians, at Demersville, in this Territory, and that the Attorney General is very anxious that the matter be carefully investigated.

I am of the opinion that the statement of Chief Eneas, forwarded by me to the Commissioner of Indian Affairs, can be relied upon, as that chief has never deceived me to my Knowledge, and I regard him as a truthful man, or I would not have gone to the trouble to present his statement to the Indian Department.

As the Chief is now out in the mountains with his people on a fall hunt, I think it would not be well to proceed before the U.S. Commissioner at Missoula, pending the convening of the United States Grand Jury, as it would not give time to hunt up the Indian witnesses that Eneas promised to furnish, nor, indeed, to find the Chief himself.

I am in receipt of a letter from the Honorable Commissioner of Indian Affairs, under date of October 14th, in regard to this case, in which he requests that I extend to you all proper aid and facilities at my command in the prosecution of your investigation. I shall be happy to extend to you any assistance you may require of me.

As Eneas and his people are now away, I think it advisable to delay the matter until the meeting of the U.S. Grand Jury. In the meantime it would be well to issue subpoenas for witnesses with date and place where you may require their appearance. If you can leave a blank for names of witnesses, I shall insert their names, and give my personal attention to the procuring of their attendance at the proper time.

General Carrington, is now at this Agency, to settle the Bitter Root Indian land question, under authority of the Act approved June 15th, 1872 (17 Stat. 227) [sic, June 5, 1872 (17 Stat. 226)] also that of March 2d 1889 (25 Stat. 187) [sic, (25 Stat. 871)], and my time will necessarily be devoted to him for a few days, after which I shall be ready to take up this matter. Please communicate your suggestions, and command me.

I am,
Yours truly
Peter Ronan
U.S. Indian Agent.

November 29, 1889
LR 34,974/1889, RG 75, National Archives, Washington, D.C.

United States Indian Service,
Flathead Agency, Montana
November 29th, 1889.

The Hon. Commissioner of Indian Affairs
Washington, D.C.

Sir:

On the 11th of November I was visited by D. B. Wilson, Captain of the 25th Infantry, and R. H. R. Loughborough, 1st Lieut. 25th Inf., who informed me that the Commanding officer at Fort Missoula was in receipt of a telegram, dated at St. Paul, Nov. 9th, 1889, in which the Interior Department informed the Secretary of War of the request of the then Governor of Montana (White) asking that troops be speedily sent to the Flathead Lake Country, in said Territory, to protect the citizens against violence feared from Chief Eneas and his band of Kootenai Indians, arising from the bad feeling occasioned by the killing of the Chief's Son, and from previous trouble between whites and Indians. The above was communicated on the 9th of November by telegraph by the Division Commander, and the Department Commander directed that officers be sent to investigate the matter and report action and the result to Headquarters, at St. Paul, Minnesota.

To show that the affair was considered serious, on the 11th of November, referring to previous dispatches on the subject the Department Commander directed to continue dispatches from Division Headquarters after the word "Indians," as follows:

Also request that the commander of the military post nearest the vicinity referred to investigate the matter, and if he finds the same to be warranted by the fact, to use such military forces as may be necessary to secure the citizens against danger of harm from the Indians.

Under instructions from the Major General commanding the Army, the Division commander directs that he take the necessary steps to comply with request of Interior Department, reporting action in the premises by telegraph to head quarters.

The Department commander directed that the Commanding officer at Fort Missoula, send without delay, an officer accompanied, if necessary, by a detachment to investigate and report the condition of affairs in the Flathead Lake region, the present state of feeling between settlers and Indians. Whether any, and what unfriendly acts have recently been done by the latter or threats made or depredations committed.

Should it be found on report of the officer, or otherwise, that immediate action is necessary to protect settlers or prevent serious trouble, you will send without waiting further orders, a sufficient force to prevent harm. Acknowledge receipt and state any information of recent disturbance or cause for apprehension as you may have, also report by telegraph action taken hereon.

This was signed by command of General Ruger, commander of the District of Dakota and official copy furnished Captain D. B. Wilson, 25th Infantry, for his information and guidance.

In my interview with the Army officers I informed them that there was no necessity to take a military detachment with them; that there was no danger whatever to be apprehended by the citizens from the Kootenai Indians, under Chief Eneas, of this reservation; that although that Chief mourned the loss of a son killed at Demersville, at the head of the Flathead Lake, supposedly by whitemen, and that although two of his tribe were hung at the same place by a mob and without a trial, and other outrages committed, through the sale of whisky to Indians, that no fear might be apprehended by the whites from that kind-hearted Indian Chief, Eneas, who devotes his influence and his energies to keep his people from getting into trouble growing out of the sale of whisky by dissolute whitemen to his poverty stricken and unfortunate band.

Not having the time to spare to accompany the officers, I requested Mr. Lambert, head farmer at this Agency, to proceed with them, and to make report to me of his observations in regard to the apprehended trouble. I have the honor to enclose said report and, also, copy of official report of the Army officers sent to investigate the matter, addressed to the Post Adjutant at Fort Missoula.

I believe that attached reports clearly Show and bear out my views in all statements made by me to the Indian Office, in my communications in regard to affairs in the Flathead region.

I have the honor to be,
Very respectfully,
Your ob'dt Serv't,
Peter Ronan
U.S. Indian Agent.

First enclosure:

Copy

Fort Missoula, Mont.
November 20th, 1889

To the Post Adjutant,
Fort Missoula, Mont.

Sir:

We have the honor to report that, pursuant to Orders 126, Post, of November 11th, we left post same day enroute to Flathead Lake country, stopped one day at the Flathead Indian Reservation, interviewed Mr Peter Ronan, U.S. Indian Agent to learn from him the extent of the troubles, all the facts regarding the disturbances, their causes, &c. and the next day continued our journey to Demersville, ten miles north of the head of Flathead Lake, the centre of the country where the alleged troubles occurred; where we arrived on the 14th Inst.

We at once put ourselves in communication with the citizens, drove around through the villages and settlement, looked up and learned as far as possible the locality of all of the Indian camps, and interviewed as many of the leading citizens and settlers possible, from all parts of the country, probably from seventy to one hundred in all, and from the various opinions and statements attainable believe the following to be the facts and true condition of affairs, viz: —

Eneas, with his band of Kootenai Indians, who have their permanent home on Dayton Creek, is now camped with his tribe, (women and children) in various places in Pleasant Valley, Smiths Valley &c. hunting for the winter. His people, as a tribe, are peaceable and law abiding and are not disposed to create trouble or disturbances in any way.

In March 1888, two men of Eneas' band were seized by the citizens of the vicinity of Demersville, accused of having killed three white men, at or near

Wolf Prairie, and after they were taken into custody by a Deputy Sheriff were again taken from him, by force, and hanged at or near that place.

Last August Eneas' son "Samuel," who was inclined to be wild and fond of liquor, became intoxicated, and when in that condition, tried to break into a house to get something to eat, as he said, and the occupants becoming alarmed, shot him.

In consequence of these troubles, although Eneas feels as though injustice was done and that it was not necessary to kill his son nor indeed the other Indians in 1888, until they had been properly tried and convicted by due process of law, has never threatened or even contemplated any violence in return. He only asks that due process of law be observed and justice be done. These troubles may have, however inculcated a spirit of revenge in some of his young and turbulent bucks, and in case of future trouble, his authority may be defied by some individuals of them.

A considerable number of renegade Kootenai, who acknowledge no tribal relations or authority, recruited probably by Stoney Indians of some character from across the British border, by troublesome bucks who, for various misdemeanors have been driven from the camps of all the peaceable indians in all the surrounding country, are reported to be encamped in various places in Tobacco plains, in Kootenai valley, and near or on the British line (and the murderers La La See and Pierre Paul, from near Ravalli, in the Flathead Reservation are said to have a refuge among them) are travelling to and fro, gambling, would be isolated cases of marauding &c.

Thus far they are accused only of killing cattle (and no specific cases of these are named) and stealing food, tearing down fences and keeping the settlers, women and children, in a state of apprehension and terror.

A large part if not all the troubles existing between the indians and whites is clearly traceable to the use of liquor by the indians and the attending idleness and dissipation.

The liquor is purchased by tramps and vagabond whites at $1.00 per bottle and sold to the indians for $2.00 and thus they make an illicit living.

The Flathead country is now almost entirely settled up, nearly every claim being taken, and the whites exceed the indians living there, or that can come there in the ratio of ten to one or more and they can, ordinarily, if their peace officers will perform their duty, keep the indians in subjection, but in consequence of the community being scattered and the settlement new, unavoidable difficulties arise to enforcing the laws. The settlers are very much scattered, the men are employed about their farms, and in the woods at their labor, and their families are necessarily left alone a great portion of the time and are, of course, in a constant state of fear and trepidation.

The opinion among the settlers seems to be, with very few dissenting voices, that there will be no general outbreak of the indians, but that whatever trouble arises if any is contemplated, will be caused by these wandering and irresponsible vagabonds, strengthened by all the troublesome young braves of the various surrounding tribes who will defy the authority of their chiefs, and that there is no danger of them taking the war path or indulging in any violent acts now — that they are in winter camps and the snow on the ground until early spring, probably last of February or early in March, when the snow has partly or wholly disappeared and the grass is again available.

For the present the settlers appear quiet and until early spring arrives, they do not, we think, apprehend any danger.

The settlers, many of them old miners and frontiersmen who are accustomed to the trials and dangers of frontier life, are extremely anxious for the presence of troops, claiming that the very presence of an armed force will strengthen them and subdue these wild and ungovernable indians, and deter them from violence, and render them less saucy and arrogant.

Very respectfully,
Your obedient servant,
(Signed) D. B. Wilson,
Captain 25th Infantry.
(Signed) R. H. R. Loughborough,
1st Lieut, 25th Infantry.

* * * * *

1st Endorsement.

Fort Missoula, Montana.
November 21st 1889.

Respectfully forwarded to the Assistant Adjutant General Department of Dakota.

I would recommend that one company from this post filled to fifty men by details from other companies, be sent into the Flathead Country the first of March next to remain two or three months, or more, as circumstances may develop and I think good results would be attained if a strong troop of Cavalry could scout the country during the same time or even longer.

(Signed) Geo. L. Andrews,
Colonel 25th Infantry, Commanding.
Fort Missoula, Montana.
November 21st 1889.

Official copy respectfully furnished U.S. Indian Agent Peter Ronan.
By order of Colonel Andrews:

Geo. Andrews,
1st Lieut. & Adjt. 25th Infantry,
Post Adjutant.

Second enclosure:

United States Indian Service,
Flathead Agency, Montana
November 23d, 1889

Peter Ronan, Esq.,
U.S. Indian Agent,
Flathead Agency, Mont.

Sir:

In compliance with your order of 12th inst.; detailing me to accompany Capt. D. B. Wilson, 25th, U.S. Inf. to the head of Flathead Lake and assist in investigating the rumored disagreement between the Indians and the white Settlers of that section of the state, I have the honor to report to you the results of my observations:

Upon reaching Demersville, the head of navigation on the Flathead river, Capt. Wilson and myself proceeded to interview the representative citizens of that place and the farmers in the vicinity. After securing the views of these people and statements of such facts bearing upon the subject in hand as they could furnish, we went to the town of Ashley and met the leading Settlers of that portion of the valley. The Statements of the majority of the inhabitants of this place and the farms adjacent, were obtained.

After a thorough investigation of all rumors I am led to believe that whatever danger exists, is to be apprehended from renegade Indians from the British Kootenai, who reside at Tobacco Plaines, something more than a hundred miles Northwest of the reservation. These Indians are non-treaty Indians and claim allegiance to the British government, while residing on American soil; I understand some 15 lodges of this same band claim a residence at the head of Flathead Lake. There are about 12 lodges of these Indians now camped with some twenty-two lodges of British Stoney Indians, on Halfmoon Prairie, in the northern part of Flathead valley. There are, in addition to these foreign Indians, two or three lodges of Eneas' band of reservation Kootenais. These latter lodges are peopled by some young men who cannot be controlled by their Chief, and are gamblers and drunkards. This comprises the number of Indians now in the Flathead valley, so far as I could learn, and consists, as stated, of British Indians, with a very small proportion of reservation Kootenais.

My reason for thinking there might be outrages committed by these Indians when spring opens, lies in the fact that they can secure all the liquor they can pay for, as has been heretofore shown, the results of which have been demonstrated in the death of "Knock-i-o," a Kootenai, about May, last, and the recent killing of "Samuel," Son of Chief Eneas, both of which occurrences have, likely enough, engendered a spirit of revenge among the young Indians of the Kootenai tribes, — and the presence of Pierre Paul and La La See, the (Indian) outlaws and murderers, among the Kootenais at Tobacco Plains. The chief of the latter tribe has been reported to me as having said that if the whites attempted to arrest either of these renegades they would have to fight him and his tribe.

I am confident that Eneas, the Chief of the Kootenais belonging to this reservation, will do his utmost to prevent the members of his tribe from entering into conflict with the whites, and that whatever danger exists is from the British Kootenais from Tobacco Plaines and Possibly, a few renegades from Eneas tribe who may escape his control. I think, however, that all danger from the small number of Indians at the head of the Flathead Lake, could be prevented by the presence of a small body of troops during this winter and next summer, at, or near, the town of Demersville.

Very respectfully submitted,
Henry R. Lambert,
Agency Farmer.

April 11, 1890

LR 11,564/1890, RG 75, National Archives, Washington, D.C.

> Editor's note: In 1889 U.S. Army troops were sent to the Upper Flathead Valley to help prevent conflict between Indians and white settlers in the area. The contest was complicated by cultural differences, alcohol, racism, and resource competition. In spring 1890 the U.S. Army sent troops to the area in a further effort to keep the peace.[17] The troops had a musical band that entertained the local whites at Demersville.[18] According to Ronan's telegram of July 21, 1890, and his August 1, 1890, letter,[19] the troops joined the white people from Demersville in surrounding the Kootenai village at Elmo and demanding at gun point that Chief Eneas produce several Kootenai charged with killing white people. The accused were not at the camp. Eneas complained that local white authorities were not interested in punishing white people who had killed Kootenai Indians, including his son. Eneas kept his temper, despite the provocations from the invading white posse and army troops, and he made sure the episode did not explode into violence.

United States Indian Service,
Flathead Agency, Mont.
April 11th, 1890.

The Hon. Commissioner of Indian Affairs
Washington, D.C.

Sir:

A detachment of troops consisting of fifty men, besides officers, under command of Captain D. B. Wilson, of the 25th Infantry, are now marching through this reservation, on their way to the Flathead Lake region, there to establish a camp for the Summer, near Demersville, the scene of so many complaints in the past few years, between the white settlers and the Indians, owing in a great measure to the sale of liquor to the latter. On the 29th of November, 1889, I had the honor to report to you the matters which led up to the ordering of troops to Demersville. Under that date I also enclosed copy of report of military officer, and the report of H. A. Lambert, farmer at this Agency.

The troops now on the reserve are colored men, and their march to Demersville will be through this reservation for a distance of about seventy miles. The Indians, and especially Chief Eneas, of the Kootenai tribe, have requested me to accompany the command on its march through the reservation, with an interpreter. Chief Eneas, also desires to hold a cou[n]cil with the officers in command when they reach his encampment at Dayton Creek, where he desires to make known his side of the controversy between the Lake country settlers and the Kootenai Indians. Captain Wilson has also requested me to accompany his command at least to Dayton Creek, which is the home of Chief Eneas and some sixty miles north of this Agency. In compliance, I shall leave with a special interpreter, this morning as the Agency interpreter cannot be spared at this time. The orders of Captain Wilson also embrace instructions to co-operate with the Agent in the arrest of Pierre Paul and La La See, the Indian outlaws and murderers, to be turned over to the civil authorities for trial if arrest is made. The outlaws are watchful and no doubt will take to the mountains upon learning of troops being on the reserve.

Trusting my action in the premises will be approved by the Hon. Commissioner of Indian Affairs.

I am, very respectfully,
Your obedient servant
Peter Ronan

July 21, 1890

LR 22,262/1890, telegram, RG 75, National Archives, Washington, D.C.

Editor's note: On July 22, 1890, the Commissioner of Indian Affairs instructed Ronan to make a full investigation of the Kootenai-white conflict in the Upper Flathead Valley.[20]

July 21, 189 [sic]
Arlee, Mont.

Comr Indian affairs
W, DC

Rumors reached me through Indians that Kootenains of this reserve were surrounded by U.S. troops & Citizens & made demand on Chief Enas to deliver up an alleged murderer. agency farmer now taking Census writes under date eighteenth Inst from Stigmatius [St. Ignatius] Mission. I learn forty white men started from head of flathead lake on horse back for Kootenai Camp & about forty soldiers took steamer for same place surrounded Camp before daylight & surprised Indians. officer in Command demanded murderer. Chief pointed the Indiancy [sic] & said if you take him will fight. when you turn over the murderer of my son & Antoine who Killed finley I will give up to you every one of my Indians who have Killed any white men, otherwise I will not & if you attempt to take them I will fight. Officer told Enas he would give three days to deliver murderer otherwise would take him. Troops & Citizens then returned to head of Lake. I recd no notification of trouble from other citizens or soldiers but believe agency farmers Information substantially true. Kootenai Camp sixty miles from here. telegraph shall I proceed to Camp & Investigate. await instructions.

Ronan
Agt.

August 1, 1890

LR 24,311/1890, RG 75, National Archives, Washington, D.C.

Editor's note: Ronan argued that much of the Kootenai-white conflict in the Upper Flathead Valley resulted from the sale of whiskey to Indians and the unwillingness of the white authorities to prosecute white men who killed Indians. Cases of Indians killing white men, however, were widely publicized and vigorously pursued.[21] As Ronan reported, in July 1890 a posse of white men invaded the reservation, surrounded the Kootenai camp, and threatened Chief Eneas. With remarkable restraint, Eneas pointed out that the accused murderers were not in the camp, requested justice for Indians killed by white men, and avoided any reaction that could escalate into violence.[22]

See Ronan's August 14, 1890, annual report where he repeated his request for justice for the murder of Chief Eneas' son.[23]

William Houston was elected Missoula County Sheriff in the fall of 1889 because he promised to use aggressive tactics in the hunt for Indians accused of killing white people.[24]

United States Indian Service,
Flathead Agency, Mont.
August 1st, 1890.

The Hon. Commissioner of Indian Affairs
Washington, D.C.

Sir:

Referring to my telegram to you dated at Arlee, July 21st, 1890, which called attention to rumored trouble between Kootenai Indians and settlers at the head of Flathead Lake, and to your reply by wire, of July 22d directing me to proceed to the Camp and investigate cause of trouble, and to use my best efforts to prevent a conflict between whites and Indians, I now have the honor to report as directed:

For a number of years my reports to your office have spoken of ill-feeling prevailing between the settlers at the head of Flathead Lake and a band of Kootenai Indians of the reserve that occupy land midway of the Lake and adjacent to the settlements of the whites. Whiskey has been sold to the Indians by the whites and resulted in several rows in which some Indians were Killed by the latter, and among them the son of Chief Eneas, of the Kootenais; two of the Chief's Indians were also hung by a mob of settlers for alleged murder, without trial or recourse to law. Pending an investigation by the Missoula County Grand Jury, into the Killing of the son of the Chief, it adjourned three days before I was able to bring the Chief and his Indians witnesses into court. These unfortunate circumstances have shaken faith in the mind of the Indians, as to justice having been done them in the Courts, and murders and outrages have been Committed by the Indians in retalliation [sic]. I trust this state of affairs will be brought to a close by prompt arrest and speedy punishment of Indian, as well as white, law breakers.

The recent trouble which I was ordered to investigate may be stated as follows:

On last 4th of July, at a celebration at Eagan, some Indians got drunk and quarrelled among themselves. In the scuffle a gun went off in the hands of an Indian named Antoine, who was trying to arrest another Indian named Finlay. The slayer was arrested by the whites and taken to Demersville for trial. He became frightened, fearing that he would be lynched, and stated to a deputy sheriff who had him in charge, that he Knew he was going to be hung and had a confession to make. He stated that another Indian named Pascal, told him of the murder of a whiteman last spring, and pointed out to him where the body was concealed. Before a number of witnesses the Indian repeated his narrative. A party was then organized and taking the Indian with them proceeded to the spot where the body have been buried, and found the skeleton and clothes. Intense excitement was created among the white people at Demersville, when the crowd returned with the skeleton and clothing.

Antoine stated that the man was passing along the road on horseback and was met by a party of Indians. The Indians asked for whisky and the man gave them some out of a bottle. The bottle was returned to him and he started away, when Pascal shot him in the back, Killing him instantly. He also stated that the murder was committed in revenge for the previous Killing of the son of Eneas, the Kootenai Chief, by whitemen. A large sum of money, the Indian said, was found by the murderer in a money belt around the dead man's waist. A Coroner's jury was called and an inquest held over the remains and a verdict rendered that the unknown man came to his death by Pascal, according to the evidence of Antoine.

The citizens then organized to the number of about fifty determined to surround the Kootenai village and to capture Pascal and other Indian criminals that might be found there. It was arranged to start at seven o'clock, p.m. with a deputy sheriff and the citizens as a posse. A company of troops, under Command of Captain Sanborne of the 25th U.S. Infantry, who are encamped at Demersville, concluded to go to the reservation, with this party, as the Commanding officer has orders to arrest Pierre-Paul and La La See, two other reservation Indians accused of the murder of whitemen. On arrival of posse of citizens, the Indian Camp was surrounded and a demand made for the surrender of the murderers. Chief Eneas informed the leader that the Indians asked for were not there, and invited those who could identify them to search the camp. The posse then awaited arrival of the United States troops, who came about two hours after the arrival of the armed citizens. It being clearly ascertained that the Indians wanted were not in the camp, the troops and citizens returned to Demersville.

In accordance with your telegram of July 22d, I proceeded to the Foot of Flathead Lake by team, and from thence took steamboat. The high sheriff of Missoula County joined me on the steamer and we both proceeded to Demersville. On arrival there we found the town in wild commotion, and it was stated to the sheriff and myself, than an organization of two hundred men was formed, and that on Wednesday, the 30th of July, they would march to the Camp of the Kootenai Chief, on Dayton Creek, and capture the culprits even if it involved a fight with the chief and his band. If the Indians sought for were not found at the Kootenai camp then they would march to St. Ignatius Mission, where the Church and Indian schools are situated and where the annual feast of St. Ignatius would be celebrated on the 31st, and where a great gathering of Indians would be found. I informed some of the leaders that I was ordered on the ground to prevent a collision between the Indians and the whites; that a march of a mob of disorganized men would surely result in bloodshed, and would not accomplish the arrest of the outlaws, as it was evident as soon as warning came of the march the culprits would take to the mountains and escape while innocent parties would be made the victims, should a conflict occur.

The sheriff stated to the leaders that he would not take any responsibility for the action of the mob; nor would he authorize any of his deputies to do so. This settled their conclusion to give up the expedition for the present. But it was stated by the leader that a reasonable time would be given the authorities to capture the Indians accused of murder and their accomplices, or that the matter would again be taken in hand by them as they intended to hold the organization together and Compel arrest or a fight.

I sent a messenger to the Kootenai Camp and called Eneas, the Chief to meet me at St. Ignatius Mission, which he did. I demanded Pascal to be delivered up for trial for murder at Missoula, the County seat. After considerable discussion the chief said that, if Antoine, the accuser of Pascal for murder, would be brought to Missoula, as prosecuting witness, he would at once deliver Pascal to the authorities for trial. I readily acceed [sic] to this as sheriff Houston stated he would get Antoine for witness at once. I considered that by the arrest and trial of Pascal, the accused murderer of the traveller, that it would lead, in a short time, to the peacable arrest of every Indian for whom the Sheriff holds a warrant. I apprised the sheriff of the Chief's proposition, but did not yet learn if he acted upon it.

In order to settle the present difficulties between the white settlers at the Head of Flathead Lake and the Indians of this reservation, every Indian charged with crime should be arrested and tried and if guilt is proved, punished to the full extent of the law. The Indian Police are afraid to make the arrests as they claim the outlaws have a small number of followers who have given them warning that revenge on themselves and families will follow. The Chiefs are weak and afraid to act — in short the great majority of Indians who are peaceful and law abiding have been terrorized by a few gamblers and outlaws, who harbor and protect the criminals. It is my opinion, that those outlaws should be taken by the lawful authorities, no matter at what cost, or it will result in a conflict that will be ruinous to the civilized, the progressive and the inoffensive members of the confederation of Indians occupying this reservation and also, result in bloodshed of innocent white travellers and isolated settlers who will be made the victims of revenge, which is the Indian mode of warfare.

Very respectfully
Your obedient servant,
Peter Ronan
U.S. Indian Agent.

October 31, 1890

LR 34,724/1890, RG 75, National Archives, Washington, D.C.

Editor's note: See the annotation to Ronan's October 30, 1891, report on the survey of the northern boundary of the reservation for background on this problem.[25]

On December 12, 1890, Ronan was authorized to employ a farmer for the Kootenai who would live near the Kootenai village and be paid $60 a month.[26] Ronan chose Robert H. Irvine, a mixed blood of white and Snake descent who spoke Kootenai and operated a cattle ranch on Crow Creek in the Mission Valley.

United States Indian Service,
Flathead Agency,
October 31st, 1890.

Hon. Commissioner Indian Affairs
Washington, D.C.

Sir:

Having lately returned from a trip to the Kootenai Indian village, at Dayton Creek, and West of the Flathead Lake, where I was ordered by you to investigate and report upon the boundary survey of Deputy U.S. Surveyor E. P. Harrison, a full report of which I forwarded to your office. Having had an opportunity to council and consult with Eneas, the Chief of this unfortunate band, who now realizes the deplorable condition of his people, and who expresses his willingness to enter into any arrangement looking to the bettering of their condition, I shall here outline the proposition I made to him, with your approval, and he fully agrees and seems delighted at a proposal which, I believe, in a short time will place himself and his band in comfortable independence.

Dayton Creek empties its waters into the Flathead Lake a few miles south of the center of that Lake, on the West side, and about sixty miles North of the Agency. Here a detached band of the British tribe of Kootenais made their homes long before the Stevens treaty was made, and here Governor Stevens found them when he entered into treaty with the Indians of this reserve, and included the band as a portion of the Confederation of Flatheads, Pend 'd Oreilles and Kootenais who were to occupy this reservation. . . . . Eneas, the Chief of this band, is a good meaning man, and if encouraged, will do all in his power to keep his Indians from wandering about, and to insist upon them turning their attention to farming and stock raising and other civilizing pursuits. I agreed to place a farmer in their settlement, there to permanently reside, whose duty it shall be to assist them next winter in getting out rails, and to fence individual farms for families who may desire to cultivate the land next Spring. To furnish seed and have the farmer teach them how to plant, cultivate and harvest. To furnish plows and other implements of labor, and if the crops warrant, to send a threshing machine to thresh their grain next season.

If the survey upon which I reported be not allowed to cut off the meadow and agricultural land claimed by the Kootenais from time immemorial, and if the Commissioner will permit me to employ a farmer, one whom the Chief has already recommended — a thrifty halfbreed farmer of this reserve, by the name of Robert H. Irvine, who was born among them — speaks the language, reads and writes English to a limited extent, and of good moral character. This man is willing to turn his own farm over to his brothers and take his family to the Kootenai village, and accept the position of farmer for them. I repeat, if I am ordered and assisted to carry out this plan, I shall have the Kootenai in an improved condition in a short time.

At the present term of court at Missoula, two of this tribe were sentenced to be hanged for murder. The chief and his band keenly feel their degredation, and if an energetic movement is made at once as above outlined, instead of scattering out in hunting and gambling parties, I can place these Indians at work fencing in farms and preparing for a season of labor.

On account of the large number of settlers who are now crouding [sic] into the country at the head of the Lake, it is necessary to have a reliable man at the Kootenai village, on the border of the reserve, to look after the interest of the Indians in other respects as well as to teach them to farm. The Northern portion of the reservation is one of the finest cattle ranges in the Northwest, and Chief Eneas complains that settlers at the head of the lake, drive great herds of cattle in the night to the boundary of the reserve and let them stray over and turn them loose on the reservation. This could be prevented by the farmer, who could take the Indians and round up and drive the cattle back across the border until trespassers would tire of having their bands herded and driven by Indians. Where cases have been brought against settlers having cattle on the reserves, notably at the Blackfeet reservation, the case was thrown out of court on the plea that stock could not be prevented from straying on the reserve unless the same was fenced.

Trusting this matter will receive your kind attention,

I am very respectfully,
Your obedient Servant,
Peter Ronan,
United States Indian Agent.

October 30, 1891

LR 39,947/1891, RG 75, National Archives, Washington, D.C.

Editor's note: The survey of the northern boundary of the reservation had caused problems for Ronan and the tribes and friction with neighboring whites for almost a decade. Much of the conflict had centered on grazing trespass by white owned cattle. In the twentieth century the United States Court of Claims agreed that the survey of the northern boundary of the reservation had been in error.[27] Since the Kootenai had traditionally used some of the land in question for hay and were starting grain farms on the land, Ronan requested permission to issue off-reservation allotments to the Kootenai. On September 7, 1891, the Commissioner of Indian Affairs instructed Ronan to make the allotments.[28] On October 30, 1891, Ronan reported making the allotments and filing the claims with the local land office. In October 1891, the Kootenai occupied the land, had built fences, and had planted grain.

In December 1891, however, armed white men from the head of the lake "jumped" the allotments and forced the Kootenai farmers off. Despite the provocations, Chief Eneas and the other Kootenai leaders were able to convince the younger men to pursue their claims through the white legal system rather than violence. The threats and aggression came just as a delegation of Bonners Ferry Kootenai were visiting Dayton Creek to consider removing from northern Idaho to the Flathead Reservation. The conflict attracted national attention, but a United States Marshal was able to remove most of the white squatters by the end of the year.[29]

The conflict over the Dayton Creek allotments occupied Ronan for the rest of his life. Two white men, Clarence E. Proctor and John Casey, were particularly diligent in finding legal arguments to advance their claims to homesteads in the contested area.[30] The whites dragged out the proceedings in the land office for years and harassed the Kootenai farmers until in 1904 the government abandoned its promise and pressured the Kootenai into relinquishing their allotments.[31]

One of Chief Eneas' sons and successors, Koostahtah, was able to protect his allotment from the aggressive white settlers north of the official boundary, but the other Kootenai allottees were driven off their land. Finally in 1904, Koostahtah, the only Kootenai farmer left in the area, was surrounded by hostile white neighbors. Given the unwillingness of the government to fulfill its promise to protect the rights of the Kootenai allottees, Koostahtah decided to relinquish his allotment and move south of the boundary line.[32]

United States Indian Service,
Flathead Agency,
October 30th, 1891.

Hon. Commissioner Indian Affairs
Washington, D.C.

Sir:

Referring to "Land 31598 — 1891," dated at Washington, September 7th, 1891, in which it was stated that my communication of the 25th of August, received your attention, wherein I reported that I visited, at the request of chief Eneas and his head men, the Kootenai Indians residing at Dayton Creek, on the Flathead reservation, in order to fully report to your office, upon their request, in regard to certain lands which they honestly considered as rightfully belonging to them under treaty stipulations and which they have always occupied.

You referred also to the fact that I stated that the decision of your office, rendered November 10th, 1890, relative to the boundary of the reservation was announced January, 1891; that it was fully explained to them that it was impossible to accept other boundaries than those clearly defined in the treaty of July 16, 1855; that I endeavored to convince them that the line as run by Deputy Surveyor Harrison, was in the strictest accordance with the provisions of the treaty; that I then urged upon the Indians the necessity of securing their claims to the lands occupied by them by fencing and improving the same; and that they believed they were entitled to the lands lying West of Flathead Lake and North of Clarkes Fork of the Columbia river, segregated from the reservation by the survey of the said Deputy Survey, under his contract dated

April 18, 1887.

I further stated that in obedience to my request, seventeen heads of families, over 21 years of age, of the Kootenai tribe of Indians commenced fencing and improving the lands claimed and occupied by them outside of the reservation boundary as designated by the Harrison survey; that upon my recent visit to these Indians I made personal investigation in regard to such claims; that I found the Indians whose names I furnished had not only fenced to some extent the lands claimed, but had also, on some tracts, planted small crops of grain and were then engaged in harvesting the same; that they were anxious to be assured that their lands would not be taken from them by either the Government or the whites who are now ready to "pounce" upon them.

In accordance with my request to be advised as to the proper steps to take in order to save these Indians their homes and to assist them in acquiring title to the same you have to State:

"1st. That you will at once forward a description of the lands claimed by the said Indians to the local Land office of the District in which the lands are situated, and call attention of the local Land Officers to the General Land Office circular relative to lands in the possession of Indian occupants, issued October 27, 1887, whereby Registers and Receivers are every where instructed to peremtorily [sic] refuse all enteries [sic] and filings attempted to be made by other than Indian occupants upon lands in the possession of Indians who have made improvements of any value whatever thereon (copy furnished[)].

"2d. As the lands referred to are non-reservation lands, and as the Indians were residing thereon at the date of the approval of the General Allotment Act, February 8th, 1887, they should be allotted to the Indians under the 4th Section thereof, as amended by Act of February 28th, 1891 (26 Stats., 794.)

"You will therefore at your earliest convenience proceed to that locality for the purpose of assisting these Indians in making applications for allotments under the said Acts, (copies enclosed[)].

"I enclose also for your information and use in connection with this work, copy of circular issued September 17th, 1887, by the Department, showing what is necessary to be done, how to proceed, and the proof required under the Act first named, and copy of circular issued by the Department July 2d, 1891, setting forth the amendments to the General Allotment Act as made by Act of February 28, 1891.

"You will observe from the Act and circular last referred to that each Indian whether adult or minor, married or single, is allowed, if entitled to an allotment 80 acres each, and furnishing the proof required, if there is sufficient land subject to allotment in that vicinity. If there is not enough land for that purpose, you will first allot to heads of families, in tracts of eighty acres each, and next to worthy and industrious young men, then if there is still land left you will pro rata the same among the minor members of the families referred to in tracts of not less than forty acres each, and aid them in making application for allotment of the same.

"As above stated if the lands applied for or any legal sub-divisions thereof are valuable only for grazing purposes, the same may be allotted in double quantities, and you will carry out this provision of the Allotment Acts, if it is ascertained there is enough land to do so.

"If the lands are unsurveyed, the applications should contain a description of the same by metes and bounds beginning with some natural object, or a permanent artificial monument or mound set for the purpose, or in such other manner as to admit of its being readily identified when the lines of the official survey come to be extended.

"When the applications shall have been made, you will deliver the same to the local land officers of the district wherein the lands are situated for certification by the Register, to the effect that there is no prior valid adverse claim to the lands applied for and described in each application, and to be forwarded by them to the General Land Office for Consideration and action."

In accordance with foregoing instructions, on the 18th day of September, 1891, I proceeded to the Kootenai village, on Dayton Creek, on this reservation, where I held council with Chief Eneas of the Kootenai Indians, and his band. After listening to the interpretation of my instructions from your office in regard to allotments of lands outside of the Northern boundary of their reservation, as surveyed by Deputy Surveyor Harrison, the Chief expressed for himself and his Indians, their gratitude to the Government and the Indian Office, for being allowed to get title, and to occupy the lands which they always believed to belong to them in accordance with the provisions of the treaty of 1855, but cut off on account of misunderstanding as to the exact point half way in latitude between the Northern and Southern extremities of the Flathead Lake. The Indians, always claiming the point, to be some six miles further North, until an actual survey decided the line as running very near to the Kootenai village, on Dayton Creek, and cutting off from them land which they and their fathers always claimed to be inside of the Northern Boundary of the Flathead reservation.

On the 23d of September, I commenced making the allotments, as designated by the Indians, to the following list of claimants, all being over twenty-one years of age and the head of a family.

No. 1. Antoine Dominic, 160 acres for Grazing purposes.
No. 2. Philip Kunikuka 80 acres for Farming purposes.
No. 3. Abraham Kanmekolla, 160 acres for Grazing purposes.

No. 4. Mat Kowiltawaam 160 acres for Grazing purposes.
No. 5. John Kallawat 160 acres for Grazing purposes.
No. 6. Patrick Kitcowholakoo, 80 acres for Agricultural purposes.
No. 7. William Kanklutepleta, 160 acres for Grazing purposes.
No. 8. Joseph Chuakenmum 80 acres for Agricultural purposes.
No. 9. Custa Smoketmalsukes 160 acres for Grazing purposes.
No. 10. Patrick Koskolt, 160 acres for Grazing purposes.
No. 11. George Kolkonee, 160 acres for Grazing purposes.
No. 12. Paul Chatchadoman 160 acres for Grazing purposes.
No. 13. Joseph Jean Jan Graw 160 acres for Grazing purposes.
No. 14. Bazile Tatscum 160 acres for Grazing purposes.
No. 15. Francis Nacksaw 160 acres for Grazing purposes.
No. 16. Malta Sechkolke 160 acres for Grazing purposes.
No. 17. Isaac Paul 160 acres for Grazing purposes.
No. 18. Lemo Wahomne, 160 acres for Grazing purposes.
No. 19. Jena Jan Graw, 160 acres for Grazing purposes.

This number of allotments to heads of families, being all the lands which Kootenai Indians claimed, or asked for, outside of the point half way in latitude between the Northern and Southern extremities of the Flathead Lake, as established by Deputy Surveyor Harrison, who ran the line due West therefrom. I trust, as the lands in question were unsurveyed at the time I made the allotments, that no prior valid adverse claim to the lands applied for and described in each application, will be made or substantiated. This allotment will have the effect to satisfy the Indians that no attempt has been made by the Government, in making the survey, to take from them any land that they have heretofore claimed or occupied in the honest belief that such land was inside of the boundary of the Flathead reservation.

Being advised that Non Mineral Affidavits required to be made before either the Rigister or Receiver of the Land District in which the land is situated, or before the Judge or Clerk of any Court of Record having a seal, I proceeded to Missoula, and applied to Judge Marshall, of the Circuit Court of Montana for the appointment of Eugene Humbert, as Deputy Clerk of said Court, with power to take Indian depositions, in order that the seal of the Court might be attached, without bringing the Indians, applying for allotments, either before the Register and Receiver of the local Land Office or a Clerk of a Court having a seal. This was done in the interest of economy as the Indians making applications, according to my information would be required to appear in person to make affidavit "either before the Register or Receiver of the Land District in which the land is situated, or before the Judge, or Clerk of any

Court of record having a seal." Transportation would involve a distance by horseback or wagon, and by rail, of about one hundred miles, while subsistence etc., etc. for the Indian applicants would make the bill of expense a large one.

In the Second place the Chief especially requested that the Allotment papers be made legal without bringing the applicants to the town of Missoula, and thus avoid the annoyance which the temptations of the place and its surroundings might produce among the Indian applicants for title to their lands. The appointed Deputy Clerk of the Court accompanied me to the Indian village and witnessed their marks. I have the honor herewith to enclose receipt from the Register of the local Land Office for said applications and also vouchers covering expenses in the execution and completion of this work, and have the honor to be

Very respectfully
Your obedient Servant
Peter Ronan
United States Indian Agent.

Enclosure:

Copy of notice

To whom it may concern

I claim this land as an Indian homestead, from this post or tree North one mile and east and west one Quarter of a mile. taken under instruction of the Commissioner of Indian Affairs to Peter Ronan, U.S. Indian Agent dated Sept 7th, 1891.

Antice Dominick
his X mark

witness
Peter Ronan, U S Indian Agent
Robert Irvine.

November 2, 1891

Excerpt from Peter Ronan to Commissioner of Indian Affairs, November 2, 1891, LR 40,207/1891, RG 75, National Archives, Washington, D.C.

Never, in the history of this reservation, have the Kootenai Indians before brought grain to the Agency mill to be ground into flour. Last week several teams arrived laden with wheat raised by the Kootenai Indians at Dayton Creek. The distance of the travel is over sixty miles, but the Indians made the trip with loaded teams in six days, crossing the Pend 'd Oreille river on ferry boat. Chief Eneas was much elated at the acchievement [sic] of his Indians in raising and delivering wheat at the mill to be converted into flour. He accompanied the wagons to the Agency. I expect with proper encouragement, that the Kootenai Indians hereafter will produce good crops of grain and vegetables. They feel encouraged and pleased that the question of a settlement of title to the land North of the boundary of the reservation has been undertaken by allotting it to them, a special report of which I have this day forwarded to your office.

December 14, 1891

LR 45,207/1891, RG 75, National Archives, Washington, D.C.

> Editor's note: Federal Indian policy during the late 1880s attempted to consolidate scattered bands of Indians onto reservations or provide off-reservation allotments under the Dawes Act of 1887. The Bonners Ferry Kootenai land claims along the Kootenai River in Idaho provided continuing problems for Ronan until his death in 1893. Between 1889 and 1892 more conflict arose between the Kootenai and invading white settlers. On May 19, 1892, Ronan reported on a trip to Bonners Ferry where some of the band chose to move to Canada, others agreed to remove to Dayton Creek on the Flathead Reservation, and eight families requested off-reservation allotments in the Kootenai Valley. On July 20, 1891, Catherine [i.e., Justine] Fry had made preliminary allotment applications for her mixed blood family at the Coeur d'Alene Land Office.[33] Claims, counterclaims, and lawsuits over the lands began during Ronan's life and continued for many years after he died. The harassment extended into the twentieth century until the Bonners Ferry Kootenai had no land base remaining.[34]

United States Indian Service,
Flathead Agency,
December 14, 1891.

Hon. Commissioner Indian Affairs
Washington, D.C.

Sir:

Having learned from my messenger that Chief Eneas of the reservation Kootenai Indians at Dayton Creek, was very ill, and that pursuant to my call, most of the head-men and Indians had returned from their hunt and were ready to meet the delegation of Kootenai Indians that accompanied me from

Northern Idaho, to look at the lands and advantages offered to them to remove to this reservation.

On the morning of the 3d of December, I left the Agency. A four horse ambulance, driven by Irvin, the Kootenai farmer, conveyed Chief David and his Indians, while I followed with an Agency empoye in a road wagon. The first night was spent at the trading post at St. Ignatius Mission, and in the morning I gave the Indians an opportunity to visit the industrial school for boys and girls. Never having seen an Indian school before they were delighted and astonished to see the boys in the work shops and school rooms, applying themselves to their trades and studies, and the girls in their classes and sewing rooms.

At Crow Creek, fifteen miles beyond the Mission, the tongue of our ambulance was broken in fording the stream which was lined on either side with ice; but but [sic] we procured a farm wagon from Sophie, an Indian woman and continued on that night to the Foot of Flathead Lake. On the 7th, through floating ice, we were ferried across the Lake, and by a hard drive over a rough and rocky road for twenty-two miles, reached the Kootenai village, at Dayton Creek.

On the morning of the 8th Council was held at the house of Chief Eneas, who lay ill upon his bed. I briefly recited the instructions which were sent to me from the Honorable Commissioner of Indian Affairs, of my trip to Idaho, with the hope of bringing the whole tribe back with me to the reservation; of the opposition which I met, already reported to your office; of the final conclusion of the Idaho Kootenais to send the delegation that now accompanied me to look at the country; council with Chief Eneas and his people, and, to finally decided whether they would leave their own country, or not and accept the generous offer of the Indian Department at Washington.

Chief Eneas gave them a warm reception from his sick bed, and advised them to listen carefully to what I had to say, vouching for my long tried fidelity to the Indians, and advising them to give up their hunting grounds, now overrun with white people, and betake themselves to raising stock and cultivating the land. It was only a short time since himself and his people had adopted this policy, but if he lived he would use all of his energy to induce his people to remain at home and cultivate the land. He aluded [sic] to the fact that at that hour there were twenty-five, or thirty armed men who arrived from the white settlements at the Head of the Lake, and announced their purpose to hold the land which was allotted to the Indians near their village, claiming that it was beyond the boundary of their reserve and that the Indians had no right to it. Although his young men demanded to go out on their allotments, on equal terms, with arms in their hands, he would listen to the Agent's advice, and restrain them from interfering with the trespassers, until the Great Father in Washington was apprised of their trouble and would take measures to protect the Indians in their rights. I purchased a beef for them and left them to welcome their guests, eat and talk. The Council lasted for two days and it was finally agreed that the Kootenai Indians of Northern Idaho would remove to Dayton Creek, and take up their homes among the reservation Kootenais, first having me to promise that they would be provided with provisions and clothing, houses, agricultural implements, wagons and harness, seed, and assistance in teaching them to farm. Some of the tribe own cattle to the amount of one hundred head, and about one hundred and fifty horses. They claimed, properly, that they could not march and drive their cattle such a long distance in winter time, on account of mountain ranges and deep snow, nor in early Spring, on account of high water in the numerous streams. They asked for transportation for all who had none from Kootenai river to Kootenai station, on the Northern Pacific railroad, thirty-five miles; then by rail to Arlee, near the Agency, 155 miles; and from the Agency to Dayton Creek seventy miles. When I meet the tribe in Northern Idaho, I shall try to induce those who own Stock to remain and winter them there, and offer provisions and clothing to those who remain there and take care of the stock and in the Spring, after the floods, to furnish provisions and assistance in making the march and drive to the reservation, in Montana. The presence of a mob of whitemen at Dayton Creek, jumping the allotments made by me to the members of Chief Eneas' band, on Dayton Creek, and North of the boundary, under instructions from the Hon. Commissioner of Indian Affairs, and the fact that one of the locators had commenced cutting a ditch about three miles above the Indian village, which would turn the water of the creek from its natural course and upon the land he located and completely cut off the supply which runs through the Indian village, was an ag[g]ravating piece of business to the young Indians of the village, and it was a fortunate circumstance that I came there in time to prevent them from meeting the jumpers in open hostility.

This piece of business also had a chilling effect upon the Kootenai Indians from Northern Idaho, who had just left such scenes of land jumping by the whites from the Indians, to seek peaceful homes and an opportunity to be assisted in the support of themselves and their families on a reservation. My promise that the authorities in Washington, would settle the difficulty and do justice to the Indians as well as to the whites, and carry out every promise made to them, had the effect to assure them of protection and assistance. Soon as pressing business matters are adjusted at the Agency, I shall return to Northern Idaho with the delegation that accompanied me. A council will be held there and matters explained to the whole tribe by their representatives and myself, and I shall at once enter upon the work of removal. Herewith I enclose necessary expenses to date accompanied by vouchers.

I am very respectfully
Your obedient Servant
Peter Ronan
United States Indian Agent.

January 3, 1892

Excerpt from LR 1,154/1892, RG 75, National Archives, Washington, D.C.

Editor's note: In December 1891, Ronan was actually able to get the local government officials in Montana to support his efforts to protect the Kootenai Indian allotments just north of the reservation boundary. Unfortunately, as soon as the white official left the Flathead Valley, the trespassers returned.

The United States Marshall for Montana sent a deputy to order trespassers from Kootenai Indian land at Dayton Creek. Five of the trespassers refused to obey the Deputies instructions. In letter of recent date, the Marshall informs me that he will proceed to Dayton Creek in person, and attend to the enforcement of the law.

February 18, 1892

LR 7,313/1892, RG 75, National Archives, Washington, D.C.

Editor's note: This letter was Ronan's answer to a February 6, 1892, inquiry by the Commissioner of Indian Affairs based on a report on Flathead Agency by Inspector Benjamin H. Miller. Senator G. G. Vest of Missouri also wrote to the Commissioner to ask about any charges filed against Dr. John Dade, the Flathead Agency physician. The Commissioner accepted Ronan's defense of Dade; Robert Irvine, assistant farmer; and some of the Indian police and judges, and no further action was taken.[35]

United States Indian Service,
Flathead Agency,
February 18th, 1892.

Hon. Commissioner Indian Affairs,
Washington, D.C.
Sir:

Replying to "A" 45483 – '91, dated February 6, 1892, in which you state that you are in receipt of information in relation to certain matters at this Agency as follows:

"Agency Physician: Dr. John Dade is 64 years of age, and is scarcely equal, physically, to the performance of his duties as Agency Physician."

In reply to this I would state that Dr. John Dade was appointed to the place he now holds here originally from the Indian Office in 1886; that he has faithfully filled his position, and at the end of each fiscal year from that date, I have sent his renomination to your Department for consideration with record of his age which I suppose will be found on file in the Indian Office.

Doctor Dade is a man of excellent character — has the confidence of the Indians, and at no time to my knowledge, refused a call upon a patient, whatever the distance from his office to any point on the reserve. If his resignation is called for on account of his age I sincerely hope that a doctor may be appointed to this Agency who will be of equal moral character and as trustful to fulfilment of all duties connected with his profession when called upon by the Indians.

"Assistant Farmer: Robert Irvine, assistant, is reported as a drinking man. It is also stated that some months since he was drunk, and in consequence, became involved in a row."

Assistant Farmer Robert Irvine is a halfbreed, and upon my recommendation was appointed to assist the Kootenai Indians at Dayton Creek, which is 60 miles from this Agency, in commencing farming and other pursuits pertaining to the advancement of this much neglected tribe. How well he succeeded may be noticed from reports from this office showing that some twenty farmes were cultivated last year by this band who never before attempted to cultivate the soil, and that for the first time in the history of that tribe, after harvest last fall they hawled [sic] to the Agency a number of bushels of wheat to be ground into flour at the Agency mill, having hawled it by wagon over 60 miles. This advancement was done in a great measure through the efforts of Irvine, whom the Kootenai Chief especially requested nominated for the appointment because he talks the Indian language and the Chief reposes confidence in Irvines power to promote the interest of the Kootenai tribe in agricultural pursuits. The drinking affair was reported to me at the time, and Irvine was sent for. He acknowledged that on the 4th of July of last year he was in company with a number of white freighters and teamsters, and also halfbreed Indians; that on account of the celebration of the day, some one introduced intoxicants and he indulged; that a row commenced among the party, and that in trying to quell it he had to give one or two of the halfbreeds rough usage. They took advantage of the fact that he indulged with them and made complaint that he was intoxicated. I investigated the affair at the time and upon the agreement of

Irvine to refrain from drinking in the future continued his employment with the express understanding that he would be discharged if a knowledge of such indulgence again came to my notice.

As to the Indian Judge reported I wish to state that the occurrance took place at the same time and place, and under the same circumstances as that of Irvine. The Judge reported the affair to me in person: Said that he was induced to drink liquor on that day — that he was sorry for it, and a like occurrance would never take place with him. His explanation was so comical that I related it to inspector Miller, at the Agency, after he had listened to the complaint against this particular Judge, from a halfbreed who is wealthy and always has a grievance if things are not conducted by the Indian Judges, police and others connected with the service to suit his particular views, which I have found in many cases to be selfish ones. The explanation of the Indian was: that he came among the party of freighters teamsters and halfbreeds. He was told it was the 4th of July — inducements were offered him to drink, which he did, and came personally to report the circumstances to me, and to state that he never would again be guilty of a like transgression. In his statement he said: "I have no fault to find with the white men who gave me the liquor — no complaint to make against the halfbreeds who induced me to drink it; the only complaint I have is against 4th of July, and when I hear of him hereafter I shall stay at home!"

The reason I did not discharge the men or report the case of the farmer and the Indian Judge was because of the circumstances under which the misdemenors occurred, and the solemn promises that occasion for complaint for such conduct would not happen again.

I am very respectfully
Your obedient servant
Peter Ronan,
U.S. Indian Agent.

March 24, 1892

LR 11,675/1892, RG 75, National Archives, Washington, D.C.

United States Indian Service,
Flathead Agency,
March 24, 1892.

Hon. Commissioner Indian Affairs
Washington, D.C.

Sir:

Herewith I have the honor to forward within attached letters which will give information in regard to the occupation of lands by whitemen, allotted by me to certain Kootenai Indians, at Dayton Creek, under orders from your office dated September 7th, 1891. If the trouble is not soon settled it will deter the Kootenai Indians of that place from putting in any crops this year, and perhaps may lead to trouble between the white people at the head of Flathead Lake and the Indians of this reservation.

I am very respectfully
Your obedient Servant
Peter Ronan,
U.S. Indian Agent.

First enclosure:

Office of the
United States Marshal
District of Montana
Helena, Montana, March 5, 1892.

Major Peter Ronan,
Arlee, Montana.

Dear Sir:

In conversation with Mr. Weed yesterday, prior to his departure for Washington, he expressed a belief that I had no legal authority in the Dayton Creek matter, until after having received notice in writing from both Attorney General Miller and Land Commissioner Carter, and such instructions should invest me with the power of ousting the trespassers, wherever found on Government lands, whether allotted or otherwise.

After this consultation I have decided to remain quiet in the premises until I hear from Mr. Weed at Washington, which will be in a few days. I shall keep you fully advised in this matter and trust my instructions will soon be forthcoming.

With kind regards to Mrs. Ronan and family, I am,

Your very truly,
Wm. F. Furay
U.S. Marshall.

Second enclosure.

Editor's note: The handwriting was very hard to read and this is the editor's best interpretation:

Kalispell, Montana, Mar. 16, 1892

Magor Petter Ronan Esq Arle

Dear Sir

the Chiefs Eneas Son is making trouble at Dayton Creek he has threatened to Kill Dempsy in two days; and if there is not some thing done soon there is going to be trouble.

We have done Every thing in our Power to favor and be friendly With the Indians but to hold our land and and [sic] Keep other White men off of it we will have to fence and Improve it. thare is a [illegible] going Come down from Demersville that have tried to make all the Trouble boath for the Indians and White men they Could. there is No doubt but what there is two or three Indians that are intitled to land off of the Reservation. that is those that Settled on land prior to February 8th, 1887. We make no Claim on those lands. the land We Claim is land that We Can Prove a Prior Write and Settlement to any Indian and We Intend to hold it untill Sutch time as the Land Department at Washington desides against us. I have it from Washington that all we Kneed is Proof Whitch We have that our first locations Was a head of any Indian and that thare was not any Indian living on the land at the time of the alotment Feb 8th, 1887 Whitch We Can also Prove.

of Corse those Indians that have Just Claims I am Willing to help them to Prove their rites. but it is unjust for you and them to hold out that all of that land is the Indians Simply because two of them have Probly been on this land long enough to hold it and it Will Caus troube for Boath Indians and us and Probably Blood Shed by the Way they are talking and Acting now.

I Wish you Would Consider and advise about What you Can do if any thing to make Peace if you Can not do any thing We Will have to look further for Protection.

Yours C. E. Proctor
John Casey.

Third enclosure:
Copy

United States Indian Service,
Flathead Agency,
March 22, 1892.

Messrs J. E. Proctor [i.e., C. E. Proctor] & John Casey:
Kalispel, Montana.

Gentleman:

I am in receipt of your letter of March 16th 1892, relative to the threats of the Son of Chief Enas, and also in connection with your occupancy of land claimed by the Kootenai Indians, Since and before the signing of the Stevens Treaty, believing that they were inside the boundary of the reservation. Under instructions from the Hon. Commissioner of Indian Affairs dated at Washington September 7th, 1891, "As the land refered to are non-reservation lands, and as the Indians were residing thereon at the date of approval of the General Allotment Act, February 8th 1887, they should be alloted to the Indians under the 4th Section thereof, as amended by Act of Feb. 28th. 1891

(26 Stats. 794)." As the land was unsurveyed I allotted to nineteen heads of families the land pointed out to me by each of said head of families, as that claimed by them, for either agricultural or grazing purposes.

On the 23 of September, 1891, I commenced making allotments, as designated by the Indians, to nineteen heads of families.

If any land was left I was instructed to allot it to unmarried men and among the minor members of Indian families. The Chief only desired land alloted to heads of families, who would point out their claims, and he asked for no furthur allotments, out side of the boundary as surveyed by Deputy Harrison. Having followed my instructions by forwarding a description of the land claimed by the Indians to the local Land Office of the district in which the lands are situated, and called attention of the local land Officers to the General Land Office circular relative to lands in possession of Indian occupants, issued Oct. 27, 1887, whereby Registers and receivers are every where instructed to peremptorily refuse all entries and filing attempted to be made by other than Indian occupants upon lands in the possession of Indians who have made improvements of any value whatever, thereon. I believe I have no further duty to perform, and that the matter now rests with the government as to who has proper title.

The cases of attempted occupancy of the land allotted by me to the Kootenai Indians, on Dayton Creek, have been reported by the Hon Commissioner of Indian Affairs to the Department of Justice, and I am not yet informed what steps will be taken, looking to the ajustment of conflicting claims. I trust however that good sense and love of justice to all will restrain the white claimants of these lands from any act that might lead to trouble with the Indians, until the title is settled by the proper authorities. I shall use every persuasion in my power with the Indians, to keep them from committing any act against the white claimants, and ask them to patiently await a decision from the government as to their right of occupancy.

I shall at once report you[r] commucation to the Hon. Commissioner of Indian Affairs.

Trusting that this question may meet a speedy and peaceful settlement.

I am very respectfully
Yours
Peter Ronan
U.S. Indian Agent.

June 10, 1892

LR 22,582/1892, RG 75, National Archives, Washington, D.C.

Editor's note: On July 2, 1892, the Commissioner of Indian Affairs insisted the government would protect the rights of the Kootenai Indian allottees. The Commissioner of Indian Affairs also endorsed Ronan's and Joseph Catholuha's decision to drive white owned cattle off the reservation without accepting any money which the white cattlemen could interpret as payment and permission for further white grazing on the reservation.[36] See Ronan's July 25, 1892, telegram for the next escalation in the harassment of Chief Eneas and the Kootenai farmers by white trespassers.[37]

United States Indian Service,
Flathead Agency,
June 10th, 1892.

Hon. Commissioner Indian Affairs,
Washington, D.C.

Sir:

On the 3d day of this month I left the Agency for Kootenai Indian's Camp, at Dayton Creek, in response to a message received by me from Chief Eneas of that tribe, stating that he was not able to leave his bed on account of illness, and that he was anxious to consult in regard to white settlers who took possession of lands that I allotted the Indians by your instruction, under dates 23d of September to the 26th of the same month, 1891.

I reached the house of the Chief on the evening of the 5th inst., and held consultation with him and his people. The Chief stated that the day after I left his place, after making allotments to the Indians, a party of white people took possession of a number of the allotments. (This portion of his statement was fully reported to you at the time of occurance.)

The Chief continued his statement — that while some of the land jumpers were courteous and civil, they affirmed the belief that the Agent had no authority to allot land to Indians that were outside of the boundary of the reservation as surveyed by Deputy Surveyor Harrison, and expressed determination to hold their claims until disposessed by the land laws of the United States.

Others of the jumpers were boisterous and uncivil to the Indians, and seemed determined to agrivate a quarrel. I took your advice, he continued, and held my people from getting into trouble with this class of people. It was hard to do so when an Indian saw one of them run a fence around his little enclosure and defy interference from the Indians with arms in hand.

You complained to-day, said the Chief, that the Indians did not improve their farms as well as you expected this year. How could they do so? You will find a party of white men yonder, digging a ditch from Dayton Creek, which runs through our village that will shut off our only water supply. Some could not build their fences without threats of violence. I am unable to leave my cabin but my people continue to obey me and keep quiet. I sent for you to come to ask you as our Agent, who made the allotments to my people, when can my children cultivate and improve their land without being insulted and ordered from the soil they believe belongs to them?

I could only reply that their allotment papers were in the hands of the Commissioner of the General Land Office and the Indians could only await for action there. In the mean time they must remain quiet and involve themselves in no trouble, but to place their reliance upon the justice of the law governing their case, and in due time the Great father in Washington would see that justice would be accorded them.

While at the Kootenai Indian Camp I was informed that one of the most insolent characters of the would be settlers was suspected of selling whisky to the Indians. I closely watched the matter and succeeded in getting Indian evidence against him that will secure his conviction. I have placed myself in communication with the United States Marshal and expect to have the man arrested in a few days.

A cattle roundup was in progress and the Indians were divided as how to deal with owners of stock illegally grazing upon the reservation. Previous to the commencement of the roundup I gave to the chief of Indian police to serve upon cattle owners the following order:

"It is hereby ordered that all cattle illegally grazing upon this reservation be driven off by their owners on or before the 15th of July 1892. Should any such owner of stock of any description not conform to this order the cattle or other stock may by rounded up by the Indian police and driven beyond the boundary of the reserve; and each owner may expect that sufficient number from his herd will be taken by the Indians to pay for the trouble and expense incurred in such roundup and drive. This order is issued in accordance with instructions from the Honorable Commissioner of Indian Affairs now on file in this office.

Peter Ronan
U.S. Indian Ag't."

One of the Judges of the Court of Indian Offences, charged that the Indians in former years who were intrusted with the carrying out of this order quietly appropriated any money they could collect from cattle owners and left the cattle to graze upon the reserve with intention of making a similar deal each succeeding year. The Indian Judge who makes this charge is determined to rid the reservation of the cattle as well as the imposition of the Indians who heretofore handled the case. With a party of Indian police he repaired to the roundup and demanded that no payments be taken from the cattle owners for grazing, but that all cattle be driven out, and owners warned that they must not attempt to drive them back. The other Indian faction opposed this as it would probably cut off their private revenue. I was sent for and repaired to the scene of the round up at Camas Prairie; where I held consultation with Joseph Catholuha — the Indian Judge — and his men. Catholuha contended that if money was accepted for grazing, the cattle owners would again take advantage and drive their cattle back with the expectation of settling with the Indians in in [sic] the usual way the next succeeding year. I felt that Cathoulah was right and that he was in earnest in his efforts to keep trespassing cattle owners from over running the Indian ranges with their herds. I advised him to take the field with his men and gave him the following letter:

"In the Field
Camas Prairie,
June 7th, 1892

To Cattle owners:

I was present at a Council of representative Indians last night, at which Joseph Cathoulaha Judge of the Court of Indian Offences was the principal speaker. It was decided by the council that Cattle illegally grazing upon this reservation should be rounded up by owners and driven off. As the regular Indian roundup is now in progress, all white owners of cattle are invited to be present, and are hereby notified to separate their cattle from the Indian herds and drive them away. No charges will be made by the Indians for grazing on their land in the past, but they demand that no more cattle belonging to white intruders be driven upon this reservation to feed upon the Indian ranges. White people who have stock on the reserve are notified that their cattle will be rounded up by Indians, the owner notified, and if not driven off, the Agent will be required by the Indians to take legal measures to prosecute such owners under the laws governing such cases. The Indians, under the lead of Joseph Cathoulaha will see that the decision of the council will be carried out.

Signed Peter Ronan,
U.S. Indian Agent."

I have the honor to submit my report for your consideration and approval and have the honor to be

Very respectfully
Your obedient Servant,
Peter Ronan,
United States Indian Agent.

August 9, 1892

LR 29,309/1892, RG 75, National Archives, Washington, D.C.

Editor's note: No further information was found about Charles Gardner, Flathead Agency employee, or Joseph Jean Jan Graw (Gingras) or Jean Jan Graw (Gingras), Kootenai Indian allottees.

United States Indian Service,
Flathead Agency,
August 9th, 1892.

Hon. Commissioner Indian Affairs
Washington, D.C.

Sir:

On the 25th day of July I received the following letter:

"Demersville, Montana,
July 22d, 1892.

Ronan, U.S. Indian Agent:

Sir: Charles Gardner, one of your Agency employes, requests that I inform you that there is a warrant sworn out for the arrest of Chief Eneas, at Dayton Creek by one Eugene McCarthy, he claiming that the Chief ordered him off his ranche; that in case he did not vacate would Kill him. You are asked to come at once to the the [sic] scene of the difficulty.

Yours very respectfully,
Signed James Kerr,
Captain Steamer,
'State of Montana.'"

Upon receipt of quoted letter I wired to the United States Marshal:

"Information received that warrant issued for the arrest of Kootenai Chief Eneas, for threatening violence to jumper of Indian allotment at Dayton Creek. Wire your deputies to attempt no arrest until I arrive there and make investigation.

Ronan, Agent."

Received the following reply:

"Your telegram just received: Instruct all my deputies to make no arrest unless you direct.

Furay,
U.S. Marshal."

I also wired:

"Arlee, July 25th, 1892,

Commissioner Indian Affairs
Washington, D.C.

Information received that warrants issued for the arrest of Chief Eneas for threatening violence to jumpers of Indian allotments at Dayton Creek. I wired U.S. Marshal to attempt no arrest until I arrived there to investigate. Arranged to start to-morrow morning. If instructions necessary wire to Arlee, to-day.

Ronan, Agent."

Accordingly I left the Agency on the morning of the 26th of July, and arrived at Dayton Creek on the evening of the 27th.

Chief Eneas informed me that allotment No. 19, to Jean Jan Graw, under date of September 26th, 1891, and that of Joseph Jean Jan Graw No. 13, allotted on the 25th of the same month and year were occupied by whitemen who were cutting hay on each of said allotments despite the fact that on allotment 19, the Indian or halfbreed occupant had a house, barn, enclosed and cultivated field, and also a stack of hay cut from last year, of at least fifty tons. The hay on this allotment, the Indian family claim, has been cut and stacked by them for the past twelve years. Allotment No. 13, also jumped by whites, has a log cabin, a small enclosure for a garden, and the hay has been cut by the Indian family on the same for years. The Chief being unable to walk on account of rheumatism, was carried to a wagon and driven to allotment 19; not having an interpreter, he claims that he informed the men working in the hayfield, as best he could make them understand, that the land belonged to his people by years of occupancy as well as by allotment by the Government, and desired them to vacate; the whites did so, but swore out a warrant against the Chief, in the town of Demersville, before a Justice of the Peace, who sent a constable on the reservation to make the arrest. The Chief resisted the arrest by stating that he was too ill to leave his house. The Chief then sent a messenger to the Agency to apprise me of the circumstances. The trip from the Agency to Dayton Creek involves a distance of about seventy miles. The day after my arrival at that place, the Constable from Demersville again made his appearance and demanded the arrest of the Chief, stating that if he refused to accompany him, a possie of citizens were likely to march to the reserve and make arrest by force of arms. I sent for the Chief who was hawled [sic] to my camp by the Indians in a wagon. He was willing to go before the Court, but felt in his condition the trip would be death to him. Therefore, in order to preserve peace and to prevent the coming of an armed possie of excited people to the Kootenai Indian village to arrest their Chief, I volunteered to accompany the constable to Demersville, where I went before the justice of the peace who issued the warrant and signed a bond in the sum of five hundred dollars to bring Chief Eneas before his court on the 2d day of October, 1892, to answer the charge preferred against him if he were alive and able to accompany me. I returned to camp and sent the Farmer to notify trespassers on allotments 19 and 13 to appear before me at my Camp where I would try to explain to their satisfaction that they were trespassing upon Indian allotments, and that time, trouble, and expense might be saved if my advice would be listened to. A curt reply was sent that they intended to cut the hay and hold the ground unless arrested by lawful authority, and if Indians attempted to cut the hay they would have them arrested by State authority. Before appearing before the Justice of the peace at Demersville, I sent the Indian farmer out to the nearest telegraph office and wired the following:

"E. D. Weed, United States Attorney,
Helena, Montana.

Trespassers on Indian allotments refuse to vacate unless arrested by U.S. Authority. The best interest of the service and justice to the settlers demand that a test case be made by arrest of one or two trespassers. Send U.S. Marshall Furay in person. I shall remain on the ground until he arrives. No possie will be necessary. Allotments were made to Indians according to law and Department instructions. An avoidance of bloodshed demand immediate action."

Received the following reply:

"Helena, Montana
August 2, 1892.

Peter Ronan,
U.S. Indian Agent
Kootenai Camp via Arlee,
Montana.

Dear Sir:

Your telegram of the 1st inst., relating to trespassers on Indian allotments etc., with the request that U.S. Marshal Furay be requested to proceed immediately to the scene of the difficulty has been received. I endeavored to bring the matter at once to the attention of the Marshal but he seems to be out of town and his office is locked up. I am unable to find any of his deputies here. I do not know where he is. As soon as I can ascertain his whereabouts I will repeat your telegram to him and request him to comply with your suggestion.

Very respectfully
E. D. Weed,
U.S. Attorney.["]

Upon receipt of above I ordered the Indians upon the ground and set them at work cutting their hay. I asked the Justice of the Peace at Demersville to notify the trespassers not to come again upon allotments 19 and 13 under penalty of arrest. Having put the Indians in possession without the aid of the United States Marshal, whose presense I did not expect for an indefinite period, according to the letter received from the U.S. Attorney, I returned to my camp, only to receive the following dispatch, from the Kootenai Indians at Bonners Ferry in Northern Idaho:

"Bonner's Ferry, Idaho,
August 6, 1892.

Ronan, U.S. Indian Agent,
Flathead, Montana,

When will you be here? Whites are cutting the hay off of Indian locations. They ask me to telegraph for you to come and protect their property. Please answer.

R. Fry."

I wired that I shall leave the Agency for Northern Idaho on the 10th day of August, to carry out your instruction in regard to certain allotments of lands to Indians in that country: "Land 23602 — Authority 31323," under date Washington, July 7, 1892.

I expect to find locations and lands of Indians occupied by white men who will persist in cutting hay and otherwise trespassing. I therefore desire that full instructions be forwarded to me at Bonner's Ferry, Idaho, upon receipt of this letter, as to what authority I shall call upon, and what steps I shall take to give Indians that occupy their lands in Idaho, full, free and uninterupted occupancy of the same, and the right to cut their hay without molestation. Unless I have some authoritive instructions to act or to call upon State or United States authority to aid in this work my presense there will be a useless failure, and I trust that I shall be sustained by the Indian Office in doing justice to the best of my ability to the Indians as well as to the white occupants of public land, in my humble capacity of Indian Agent, acting under orders from the Honorable Commissioner of Indian Affairs.

I have the honor to be
Very respectfully
Your obedient Servant,
Peter Ronan,
United States Indian Agent.

October 8, 1892

LR 37,894/1892, RG 75, National Archives, Washington, D.C.

Editor's note: While the government made promises to protect the Dayton Creek Kootenai allottees, officials found legal technicalities to hold up enforcement and hostile white settlers continued to invade improved Indian farms. Clarence Proctor was so aggressive that he built a fence to surround an Indian farm. Apparently the federal government's response was to argue that the state courts did not have jurisdiction in the matter. The contests stood in limbo until the summer of 1893 when they flared up again. See Ronan's June 1, 1893, letter.[38]

United States Indian Service,
Flathead Agency,
October 8th, 1892.

Hon. Commissioner Indian Affairs,
Washington, D.C.

Sir:

I now desire to draw your attention to affairs at Dayton Creek, the home of the Kootenai Indians on this reservation, and, as preliminary, respectfully refer you to my report on that business dated August 9th, 1892, which will give particulars in regard to matters that lead to the following report:

It will be seen by report referred to that Eneas, Chief of Kootenai Indians, at Dayton Creek, on this reservation, was placed under arrest by a constable upon warrant issued by a Justice of the Peace, at Demersville, Head of Flathead Lake, Missoula County, Montana. I was upon the ground when the Constable made the second arrest of the Chief, (the first was claimed to have been resisted.[)] The Constable Stated that if he (the Chief) refused to accompany him, a posse of citizens were likely to move on the reservation and make arrest by force of arms. As stated in report, in order to prevent the coming of an armed posse of excited people to the Kootenai village to arrest their Chief, I volunteered to accompany the constable to Demersville, where I went before the Justice of the Peace who issued the warrant and signed a bond in the sum of five hundred dollars to bring Chief Eneas before him on the 2d day of October, 1892, to answer any charges that might be preferred against him.

In the meantime I returned to the Agency, and by letter, laid the matter before Elbert D. Weed, United States Attorney at Helena, for the District of Montana.

While this matter was under consideration, as wired to your office, I was notified to Come to Dayton Creek again, as Chief Eneas was involved in more trouble over land allotted by me to members of his tribe. Upon arriving there I found that one Clarence Proctor, who made location near Dayton Creek, was in conflict with a certain Kootenai Indian, of Chief Eneas band. Mr. Proctor claimed that he located the land before any Indian made attempt to occupy it; while the Indian claimed that he selected the place some nine years before Proctor, for a home, and before the Harrison boundary survey was made and accepted by the Interior Department, and when it was supposed to be inside of the boundaries of the reservation set aside for the Flathead Indians and

Confederated tribes. Upon such representation made to me by the Indian, at the time I was ordered to allot lands to this band, I made the allotment to said Indian. Chief Eneas undertook to prevent the employes of Proctor from building fence and otherwise improving, and as before stated, I was sent for. I explained to the Chief "that as soon as the Indian Allotment applications of his Indians shall have been transmitted to the Indian office, by the General Land Office for consideration and action, and the lands covered thereby shall have been allotted to the respective Indian applicants, upon satisfactory proof of there [sic] being entitled thereto, under existing law, steps will be taken through the proper authorities to place each allottee in possession of his lands in order that he may enjoy the full, free, peaceable and uninterrupted use and occupancy thereof."

It was thereupon agreed between Proctor and the Chief, that the former might go on with his improvements until final decision was arrived at in the proper Department. Proctor having run a fence around the Indian enclosure, it was agreed that the Indian should have free access to his field through the gate of Proctor, until the question of ownership was decided. In the meantime the Indians would not interfere with fencing and improvement by Mr. Proctor. Thus I closed the matter until title is decided in the usual way.

Most of the Kootenai Indians were out in the mountains hunting, but before going the building in which supplies were stored for the Bonner Ferry Kootenai Indians was broken into and robbed of a large quantity of supplies and articles of clothing and blankets. It was evidently done by Indians. I informed Kootenai Chief Eneas that no more supplies would again be stored at Dayton Creek, and that the Indians should have to come to the Agency hereafter to have their wants relieved.

Owing to failure of Crops this year the Kootenai Indians are without means of support at Dayton Creek, and all are now out hunting with exception of the Chief, who is suffering from rheumatism, and a few families of old people and children. The Kootenai Indians who came from Bonners Ferry, Idaho, this fall, were discouraged and few remained. They found the crops at Dayton Creek a failure; Chief Eneas under arrest for trying to prevent white trespassers from cutting hay upon land always occupied by Indians under the belief that it was inside the boundaries of the reservation, and when learned, by actual survey, to be outside of said boundary, was allotted to the Indian occupants by the Agent under a proper instruction from the Hon. Commissioner of Indian Affairs. Under such disadvantageous circumstances the Kootenai Indians of Northern Idaho that intended to settle are restless. Untill the Dayton Creek Indian allotments are finally settled, they will continue wandering between the two localities.

As the pressing necessities of Chief Eneas and his Camp required immediate relief, I made an issue to them of supplies from the warehouse at Dayton Creek.

By attached correspondence, the Hon. Commissioner of Indian Affairs will learn of the present disposition of the case of the arrest of Eneas, the Chief of Kootenai Indians of this reservation by procedure of rural Justice of the Peace.

I am very respectfully,
Your obedient Servant,
Peter Ronan,
United States Indian Agent.

First enclosure:

Department of Justice.
Office of United States Attorney,
District of Montana,
Helena, Montana.
Helena, Montana, Sept. 29, 1892.

Peter Ronan, Esq.
U.S. Indian Agent,
Arlee, Montana.

My Dear Sir: –

Your telegram concerning the arrest of the chief of the Kootenai tribe has been received. Any crime, whatsoever committed by an Indian, upon an indian reservation, is in the exclusive jurisdiction of the Federal Courts. I wired Mr. [Seth] Seth[e]n at Demersville advising him that the U.S. had jurisdiction of the matter in all probability and to defer action until further advised[.] It seems to be immaterial what the facts may be so long as the gravamen of the charge would locate it upon reservation.

I will advise you by wire or by letter of any thing further occurring in the matter referred to.

Yours respectfully,
John M. McDonald
Assistant U.S. Attorney.

Second enclosure:

Department of Justice.
Office of United States Attorney,
District of Montana,
Helena, Montana.

Oct. 3, 1892.

Peter Ronan, Esq.
U.S. Indian Agent,
Flat Head Agency,
Jocko, Mont.

Dear Sir: –

Your communication of Sept. 30th now lies before me. I have read the matter enclosed concerning your report to the Honorable Commissioner of Indian Affairs. It was determined in a case recently tried before Judge Knowles — U.S. vs. Casey, for murder, that wherever the crime was committed, either upon the Reservation, or upon an allotment made in pursuance to regulations or treaties, that the Federal Courts had exclusive jurisdiction. There were other jurisdictional questions raised and urged in that case, but were all determined in favor of the Federal Courts retaining the jurisdiction alleged. Our opinion, in the matter now before you, wherein Chief Æneas of Kootenai tribe, is arrested by Judge McFarren, is that the case is one of Federal jurisdiction and not lodged at all in that Court. I have to-day so telegraphed to Mr. McFarren, to discharge Æneas.

Yours very respectfully,
John M. McDonald,
Asst. U.S. Dist. Atty.

June 1, 1893

LR 21,139/18923 RG 75, National Archives, Washington, D.C.

Editor's note: The government promised to protect the Kootenai allotments on Dayton Creek, but in May 1893 white trespassers returned to the area. Chief Eneas complained to Ronan and worked to keep the peace. The complaint was even reported in *The Washington Post.*[39] See Ronan's October 30, 1891, letter and annotation for background on this controversy.

In this letter, and his letter of June 30, 1893, Ronan again asked the federal government to protect the allottees.[40] The enclosed letter from Judge Hiram Knowles, Ronan, and U.S. Attorney Elbert Weed suggested that the Interior Department needed to formally approve the allotments and adjust them to the recently completed land survey so the Indians could be secure in their rights. The General Land Office held up opening the affected lands to white homesteading until the Kootenai allotments were finalized, and the Justice Department authorized the Montana U.S. Attorney to enforce the Kootenai claims.[41] This is where the situation stood on August 20, 1893, when Ronan died. After Ronan's death, no one seemed to have continued the effort to remove white trespassers who jumped the Dayton Creek allotments. Chief Eneas suffered from declining health in the 1890s and died in 1900.

Despite the many promises to protect the rights of the Kootenai farmers, the white trespassers were able to drag out the legal proceedings until the early twentieth century, when the Kootenai were pressured to relinquish their allotments to the trespassers in exchange for small payments.

United States Indian Service,
Flathead Agency,
June 1st, 1893.

Hon. Commissioner Indian Affairs
Washington, D.C.

Sir:

I desire to call attention to my report from this Agency, under date of October 30th, 1891, referring to "Land 31598 — 1891," dated at Washington, September 7th, 1891, and respectfully ask that it receive attention at this time, as I am called upon to take action in regard to persistant trespassers who refuse to vacate the allotments made by me to the Indians, as stated in report to which attention is called, under orders from the Interior Department, in 1891, to make such allotments to the Indians under the 4th section of the General Allotment Act as amended by the Act of February 28th, 1891.

Last year the Indians were deterred from making improvements, or any efforts to cultivate their allotments on account of the settlement of white people upon some of the land allotted to them.

The Indians complained bitterly against such trespass. Under date of July 2d, 1892 — "Land 23582, 1892," the Hon. Commissioner wrote: "That as soon as the Indian allotment applications of the Indians referred to shall have been transmitted to this office, by the General Land office, for consideration and action and the lands covered thereby shall have been allotted to the respective Indian applicants, upon satisfactory proof of their being entitled thereto, under existing law, steps will be taken through the proper authorities to place such allottees in possession of his lands in order that he may enjoy the full, free, peaceable and uninterrupted use and occupancy thereof and you will so notify Chief Eneas."

At the time of the receipt of quoted communication it required much tact and energetic movements to prevent the young Indians from forceably removing the trespassers from the allotments. Such action on the part of the Indians would probably involve them in a fight with the settlers that might lead to bloodshed and an expensive Indian trouble. Last year after consultation with the United States Attorney for Montana, I proceeded to Dayton Creek, the home of the Kootenais, and most of the trespassers left the Indian allotments, and quiet prevailed until the opening of Spring of this year, when they returned and again took possession of Indian allotments. Exictement [sic] again prevailed among the Indians. Chief Eneas of the Kootenai tribe came to the Agency and demanded of me the peaceful possession of the allotments made to nineteen Indians of his tribe, all being heads of families and over twenty-one years of age. Fortified by the following letter from Hon. Elbert D. Weed, U.S. Attorney for Montana, dated May 11th, 1893, I left for the Indian settlement at Dayton Creek, where I arrived on the evening of the 21st of May, 1893:

"You state that these patents have not yet issued, but that the selections of land by the Indians have been duly certified according to law to the Department of the Interior. In the routine of business of that great Department, the mechanical work of preparing and issuing the patents for said lands to these Indians has not yet been attended to. Under the law, the title of these Indians to the land in question was absolute from the time the selections were made and officially certified to the proper department. The equitable title to the land has been perfect in the Indians since that time. The legal title since then has been held by the United States in trust for them, and said land and no part thereof is in any sense whatever public land of the United States. These Indians have as perfect and absolute a right to the lands in question selected by them as allotments, as whitemen would have to the lands filed upon by them under the homestead laws of the United States. Trespassers upon these allotments, be they Indians or whites, have no legal or equitable rights whatever as to said lands. I believe it to be the duty of the Great Government of the United States to protect these Indians in their rights: to guarantee to them the quiet, peaceable and unmolested possession of the lands which they have lawfully selected as their own individual property. As the duly authorized agent and representative of the government of the United States in charge of these Indians, I am of the opinion that it is your duty to see that they are protected in said rights, and that they are saved from the molestation of trespassers upon their lands. Doubtless these trespassers are men of good but mistaken intentions, and your statement of the law and rights of the Indians on the premises to them will doubtless be sufficient to cause them to cease further unlawful interferance with the rights of the Indians. In case this should not be sufficient, it would clearly be the duty of the United States Marshal to lend you such assistance as might be necessary in causing their removal and enforcement of the law."

A written notification from me to the trespassers, accompanied by a copy of the letter above quoted from the United States Attorney, brought back the verbal reply that they (the trespassers) ignored the authority of a United States Indian Agent, and would not vacate the land unless compelled by the laws of the United States. The suggestion to take the Indian police and compell them to leave the allotments did not meet with my approval for the reason that resistance upon the part of settlers might cause bloodshed in the present excited state of the Indians, and I therefore consulted the United States Attorney in person as to the advisability of ejecting the trespassers by aid of the United States Marshal, or to at once have them arrested as trespassers, and bring the matter before the Court. Having returned to the Agency by the quickest conveyance, I wired as follows:

"Arlee, May 27, 1893

To E. D. Weed, U.S. Attorney, Helena, Montana.

Can I meet you on arrival of East bound train at Helena, on the twenty-ninth. I desire to take action against trespassers on Indian lands.

Peter Ronan
U.S. Indian Agent."

In accordance with the following reply, on the morning of May 29th I took train for Helena:

"Helena, Montana
May 27,

Will meet you as requested.

Weed
U.S. Attorney."

Upon consultation with the United States Attorney, and also with the United States District Judge, Hon. Hiram Knowl[e]s, at Helena, Montana, it was determined to lay the case before the Honorable Secretary of the Interior, for consideration and action.

Herewith I have the honor to transmit through the Hon. Commissioner of Indian Affairs, said letter addressed to the Hon. Secretary of the Interior, with the hope that it may receive prompt attention.

I am very respectfully,
Your obedient Servant,
Peter Ronan,
United States Indian Agent.

Enclosure:

Office of United States Attorney,
District of Montana,
Helena, Montana.

May 30, 1893.

To The Honorable Secretary of the Interior,
Washington, D.C.

Dear Sir: —

In 1855, Governor I. I. Stevens of Washington Territory made a treaty with the Confederate Tribes of Indians, known as the Flathead, Pend' Oreille and Kootnai Indians, residing within what is now the State of Montana, and in that treaty a Reservation for said Indians was agreed upon. The lines of that reservation were not then surveyed. In 1887, a contract was made by the United States with one Harrison, a Deputy U.S. Surveyor, to survey the North boundary line thereof, and said boundary was established by him during that year. As has been explained by Peter Ronan, Agent for said Indians, in a communication to the Hon. Commissioner of Indian Affairs, Oct. 30, 1890 [i.e., 1891], the said line thus established fell some six miles farther South than expected by said Indians. In fact they claimed that the true North line of said reservation ran across the Flathead Lake some six miles farther North. With this understanding, all of the Kootnai Indians included in said treaty had made their village North of the said line as established, and South of the line as claimed by them. Small patches of this land, they had improved and cultivated. Under these conditions, the said Agent, Peter Ronan was authorized by the Commissioner of Indian Affairs to allot these lands occupied by said Kootnai Indians in severalty under the provisions of Section 4 of the Act to Provide for the Allotment of Land in Severalty to Indians, &c. Supplement to Revised Statutes of U.S., 898. In pursuance of this order, said Ronan between Sept. 23, 1891 and Sept. 26, of same year, allotted certain lands to said Indians as will be found in his report of Oct. 30, 1891, to the Hon. Commissioner of Indian Affairs. Under rules prescribed by the Secretary of the Interior, proper applications were made for these allotments, and proper affidavits of non-mineral character of the land also filed in the office of the Register and Receiver of the U.S. Land Office, District of Montana, and were transmitted to the General Land Office at Washington. By virtue of Sec. 5 of Act of February 28, 1891, Supplement to Revised Statutes of the United States, 898, these allotments may be finally approved by the Secretary of the Interior. No notice has been received by the Agent for those Indians that this had been done. During the time that this matter has been in abeyance, a number of whites have settled upon a portion of these lands so allotted. The Indians are much disturbed on this account, and ask that something be done to insure them these lands. Upon an examination of the law we have been unable to find any authority for these Indians to whom allotments have been made, to bring suit for the possession of these lands. They have not the legal title to the same. They never had the actual possession of all the land allotted to them, only portions of each allotment perhaps. Then they would be considered as severed from the mass of public lands and not subject to settlement, and suit could be brought by the United States to eject these white settlers. If the patents were issued making the United States a trustee of the legal title for the benefit of these Indians, then the way to protect them in their rights would be open and clear. Under these circumstances, we, the undersigned, would urge some action on your part in this matter to the end that trouble may be avoided. Restless whites under ill informed and incompetent advisers, will insist upon going upon some of these lands until the matter is settled. The Indians feeling that they have been promised these lands, suspect bad faith on the part of their Agent and the United States, as long as the matter remains in abeyance and whites insist on going upon their allotments.

Hoping that you will see a way to help us out of the difficulties presented,

We subscribe ourselves,

Your Obedient Servants,

Hiram Knowles, U. S. District Judge.

Peter Ronan, U.S. Indian Agent, Flathead Agency, Montana.

Elbert D. Weed, U.S. District Attorney.

Endnotes

1. "Horrible Massacre," WM, Mar. 21, 1888, p. 3, col. 3. Two other white interpretations of these events were "A Speck of War," *Helena Daily Independent,* Mar. 31, 1888, p. 4, col. 5; and "Hi Yu Skookum!," *Bozeman Weekly Chronicle,* Apr. 11, 1888, p. 1, col. 6.

2. CIA to Secretary of Interior, May 3, 1889, letterbook 183, pp. 490-91, land; CIA to Ronan, July 8, 1889, letterbook 186, pp. 456-57, land, NA CIA LS.

3. See annotation to Ronan letters, vol. 1, pp. 383-385.

4. "Indians in War Paint," *Helena Journal,* Aug. 20, 1889, p. 1, col. 1; "An Indian Outbreak Feared," *The New-York Times,* Aug. 21, 1889, p. 2, col. 1.

5. CIA to Ronan, Aug. 21, 1889, telegram, letterbook 188, p. 329, land, NA CIA LS.

6. "Mass Meeting," *The Inter Lake* (Demersville, Mont.) Aug. 30, 1889, p. 4, c. 3.

7. "The Facts in the Case," WM, Aug. 28, 1889, p. 4, col. 5; "The Kootenai Indians Again," *Inter Lake* (Demersville, Mont.), Aug. 30, 1889, p. 4, col. 3.

8. "The Red Man's Story," *Helena Journal* (daily), Oct. 25, 1889, p. 5, col. 1-2; Ronan letters, vol. 2, pp. 148-57.

9. CIA to Secretary of Interior, Sept. 28, 1889, letterbook 189, pp. 391-95, land, NA CIA LS.

10. CIA to Ronan, Oct. 14, 1889, letterbook 190, pp. 209-10, land, NA CIA LS.

11. CIA to Secretary of Interior, Nov. 2, 1889, letterbook 191, pp. 46-48, land, NA CIA LS.

12. WM, Nov. 27, 1889, p. 3, col. 2; "News From the Lake Country," WM, Nov. 27, 1889, p. 3, col. 5; "Criminal Cases in Missoula," *The Anaconda Standard,* Nov. 28, 1889, p. 4, col. 2; Ronan letters, vol. 2, pp. 111-12.

13. "Old Timer Tells Tale of Demersville Scare," *The Daily Inter Lake* (Kalispell, Mont.), Mar. 12, 1950, p. 11, col. 1-3.

14. Ronan letters, vol. 2, pp. 96-98 and 106-11.

15. "A Squaw Shot," *The Anaconda Standard,* Mar. 2, 1896, p. 10, col. 3; *Flathead Herald-Journal* (Kalispell, Mont.), Mar. 5, 1896, p. 8, col. 2.

16. *Inter Lake* (Demersville, Mont.), Aug. 30, 1889, p. 1, col. 2.

17. War Department to Secretary of Interior, Apr. 12, 1890, 11,433/1890, NA CIA LR; Thos. H. Ruger, "Report of Brigadier-General Ruger," U.S. Secretary of War, *Annual Report of the Secretary of War* (Washington, D.C.: Government Printing Office, 1890), pp. 188-89 and 191-92.

18. "A Musical Treat," *Inter Lake* (Demersville, Mont.), Apr. 25, 1890, p. 1, col. 4.

19. Ronan letters, vol. 2, pp. 142 and 142-145.

20. CIA to Ronan, July 22, 1890, telegram, letterbook 201, p. 464, land, NA CIA LS.

21. "A Horrible Discovery," *Inter Lake* (Demersville, Mont.), July 11, 1890, p. 3, col. 4; "Dead Men's Bones," *Missoula Gazette* (daily), July 14, 1890, p. 1, col. 5; "Killed for Money," *Missoula Gazette* (daily), July 15, 1890, p. 1, col. 5; "Turned Him Loose," *Inter Lake* (Demersville, Mont.), July 18, 1890, p. 3, col. 4.

22. "A Midnight Ride," *Inter Lake* (Demersville, Mont.), July 18, 1890, p. 3, col. 3.

23. Ronan letters, vol. 2, pp. 148-57.

24. WM, Oct. 2, 1889, p. 3, col. 3; G. M. Houtz, "Old-Time Flathead Tales: Some Modern Instances," *Daily Missoulian*, Oct. 10, 1937, p. 4, col. 2-3.

25. Ronan letters, vol. 2, pp. 166-68.

26. CIA to Secretary of Interior, Dec. 6, 1890, letterbook 233, pp. 300-01, accounts; CIA to Ronan, Dec. 12, 1890, letterbook 233, p. 483, accounts, NA CIA LS.

27. See Ronan letters, vol. 1, pp. 219-22.

28. CIA to Ronan, Sept. 7, 1891, letterbook 222, pp. 293-97, land, NA CIA LS; "Outside the Line," *Missoula Gazette* (daily), Oct. 2, 1891, p. 4, col. 1.

29. Ronan letters vol. 2, pp. 264-65; CIA to Ronan, Dec. 12, 1891, telegram, letterbook 227, p. 140, land; CIA to Secretary of Interior, Dec. 12, 1891, letterbook 227, pp. 131-36, land, NA CIA LS; "Drove the Indians Off," *Helena Independent,* Dec. 13, 1891, p. 1, col. 7; *The Anaconda Standard,* Dec. 14, 1891, p. 2, col. 1; "Flathead Indians Indignant," *The New-York Times,* Dec. 15, 1891, p. 3, col. 5; *Inter Lake* (Demersville, Mont.), Dec. 18, 1891, p. 2, col. 1; "The Flathead Trouble," *Helena Independent*, Dec. 22, 1891, p. 1, col. 6; "Troublesome White Men," *The Anaconda Standard,* Dec. 22, 1891, p. 1, col. 6; "From Helena," *Butte Weekly Miner*, Dec. 24, 1891, p. 8, col. 1.

30. CIA to C. E. Proctor, Kalispell, Mont., Nov. 6, 1891, letterbook 225, pp. 108-12, land, NA CIA LS.

31. CIA to Secretary of Interior, Jan. 27, 1904, letterbook 649, pp. 183-93, land; CIA to W. H. Smead, June 9, 1904, letterbook 681, pp. 351-56, land; CIA to Samuel Bellew, Oct. 22, 1904, letterbook 711, pp. 16-27, land; CIA to Bellew, Mar. 20, 1905, letterbook 743, p. 422, land, NA CIA LS.

32. W. H. Smead to CIA, Oct. 23, 1902, 64,431/1902; Smead to CIA, May 30, 1904, 36,739/1904, NA CIA LR.

33. Ronan letters, vol. 2, pp. 325-28.

34. Elders of the Kootenai Nation, *Century of Survival: A Brief History of the Kootenai Tribe of Idaho* (Bonner's Ferry, Id.: Kootenai Tribe of Idaho, 1990), pp. 7-15.

35. CIA to Ronan, Feb. 6, 1892, vol. 128, part 1, pp. 89-90, accounts; CIA to Sen. G. G. Vest, Feb. 6, 1892, letterbook 255, pp. 81-82, accounts, NA CIA LS.

36. CIA to Ronan, July 2, 1892, letterbook 240, pp. 182-85, land, NA CIA LS.

37. Ronan letters, vol. 2, p. 312.

38. Ronan letters, vol. 2, pp. 362-65.

39. "Get Thee Gone," *The Evening Missoulian,* May 16, 1893, p. 1, col. 6-7; "Flathead Indians Angered," *The Washington Post, May 27, 1893, p. 1, col. 5.*

40. Ronan letters, vol. 2, pp. 366-67.

41. CIA to Secretary of Interior, June 16, 1893, letterbook 260, pp. 351-56, land; CIA to Ronan, June 17, 1893, letterbook 260, p. 375, land; CIA to Ronan, July 17, 1893, letterbook 262, p. 98, land, NA CIA LS; "Indian Lands," *The Anaconda Standard,* July 14, 1893, p. 1, col. 3; WM, July 19, 1893, p. 8, col. 2; "Still Unsettled," *Inter Lake* (Kalispell, Mont.), July 21, 1893, p. 3, col. 3; *Flathead Herald-Journal* (Kalispell, Mont.), July 21, 1893, p. 8, col. 3; CIA to Ronan, July 29, 1893, letterbook 262, pp. 424-27, land, NA CIA LS; "Will Be Bounced," *Western Democrat (weekly)* (Missoula, Mont.), Aug. 6, 1893, p. 2, col. 4.

Peter Ronan
(1839-1893)
A Biographical Sketch

by Robert Bigart

Flathead Indian Agent Peter Ronan and the Salish and Kootenai chiefs and headmen shared some goals and were able to cooperate to reach these common objectives. In areas where they disagreed, Ronan seems to have moved slowly and generally avoided confrontations with tribal members when possible. Apparently, Ronan was able to treat Indian people with respect.

In 1883, Indian Inspector S. S. Benedict recorded the complaints of Chief Arlee and Duncan McDonald about the St. Ignatius Mission schools and the Flathead Agency and then went on to conclude: "Agent Ronan is quite popular with these Indians. They speak in high terms of his honesty, and fair treatment."[1] A short magazine article commenting on Ronan's reappointment in 1890 observed: "The Indians in his charge all like and respect him. . . He has no hobbies about the treatment of Indians and does not expect to make white men of them in a single generation." This article, probably written by journalist E. V. Smalley, summarized Ronan's low pressure approach: "He never tries to boss them except when necessary to preserve order and keep things moving in the right way."[2] In 1895, Inspector P. McCormick noted that Ronan had been more popular with the tribal members than his successor, Joseph Carter, because Ronan humored the Indians more than Carter did.[3]

Despite Ronan's ability to respect Indian people and work with tribal leaders in areas where their goals overlapped, he was very much a late nineteenth century American. He accepted the white American ideology of the superiority of "civilized" over "savage" life and saw his mission as helping the Salish and Kootenai people progress beyond their "uncivilized" and "savage" traditional lifestyles. Many tribal members supported the St. Ignatius Mission schools because they taught the students English literacy, mathematics, and useful economic and trade skills. Ronan agreed that these practical benefits of white education were good, but also saw education as an antidote to "the demoralizing influence of Indian home surroundings."[4] For Ronan and most nineteenth century Americans, white American society was civilized and good; tribal life and values were savage and bad.

As agent, Ronan frequently argued in favor of tribal requests and interests in his correspondence with the Office of Indian Affairs. One example was the northern boundary of the reservation which nineteenth century surveys located several miles south of the line recognized by the Elmo Kootenai. Ronan requested that the Kootenai version of the boundary be recognized over the United States Geological Survey line. The Commissioner of Indian Affairs insisted on using the official survey.[5] Ronan's defense of tribal members might not have met twenty-first century standards, but one anti-Indian newspaper correspondent in 1889 accused him of being "not only an eager champion of the aborigines" but of being "activated by a prejudice against those of his own color."[6]

The two areas where Ronan and most tribal members had complimentary goals were (1) developing agriculture and ranching on the reservation to take up the economic slack caused by the loss of the buffalo and the decline of other wild game, root, and berry resources; and (2) keeping the peace on the reservation and not giving the U.S. Army or the Missoula County Sheriff excuses to intervene in reservation affairs.

A continuing aggravation for the chiefs and Ronan was the problem of uneven justice in late nineteenth century Montana. Cases of Indians accused of murdering white men were pursued vigorously by the white justice officials and the courts, but those involving Indian people murdered by whites were largely ignored. Four Indians convicted of murdering white men, mainly on Indian testimony, were hung in Missoula on December 20, 1890. The murderers of Chief Eneas' son in Demersville and Chief Michelle's relatives in eastern Montana about the same time were never caught or punished. Ronan wrote to Washington, D.C., frequently about the problem, but his calls for equal justice were not answered.[7]

One of the more important contributions Ronan made to the tribal economy on the reservation was to postpone the imposition of the General Allotment Act on the reservation for twenty years. The new policy provided for each tribal member to receive an individual allotment or portion of reservation land formerly held in common by the tribes. The policy was an attempt to forcibly convert Indian tribal hunter/gatherers to small independent farmers on the Euro-American model. Ronan personally believed in the allotment policy, but his opposition to forcing allotment on the reservation delayed it for twenty years from about 1890 to 1910. Federal policy changes during the early twentieth century progressively weakened the trust protection of the allotments, but since the protection of the allotment patents expired after 25 years under the policy, an 1890 allotment would have resulted in even fewer restrictions on the sale of tribal member lands during the 1910s and 1920s. Since the reservation was not opened until 1910, it meant that the trust protection was set to expire during the 1930s, when government policy changed and continued the trust status indefinitely. Ironically, Ronan's avoidance of conflict with the tribes protected the tribes, despite his personal beliefs about the allotment policy.

Peter Ronan was born on June 1, 1839, at Antogomish, Nova Scotia, Canada.[8] He attended a village school in Nova Scotia before his family moved to Rhode Island when he was thirteen years old. At fourteen he was apprenticed at a print shop in Rhode Island. When he was seventeen he became foreman of the book and job printing office of M. B. Young, Providence, Rhode Island. Between 1854 and 1860, he worked as a compositor for a Dubuque, Iowa, newspaper. For two years following the Pike's Peak gold rush he prospected in the Rocky Mountains, and then he returned to Kansas to work as a partner in a Democratic newspaper. After being caught up in the political turmoil surrounding the Civil War, in 1863, Ronan headed to Alder Gulch or Virginia City in what became Montana. Ronan spent several years in mining before starting a series of newspapers in Virginia City and Helena with various partners, including Martin Maginnis, who was later to become his political patron. Ronan's newspaper was burned out by the Helena fires of 1872 and 1874 and he returned to mining. He was under sheriff of Lewis and Clark County when he was appointed as Flathead Indian Agent in 1877. His twin interests in mining and journalism continued as he speculated in various mining ventures during his years at the Jocko Agency and exhibited his journalistic skills in his voluminous correspondence as agent.

Ronan had a reputation for honesty and in 1890 the *Northwest Illustrated Monthly Magazine* noted, "The Major has served a long time at the [Flathead] agency and is one of the few Indian agents who have made no money.[17] When Ronan died at the Jocko Agency on August 20, 1893, he left assets in Missoula County appraised at $5,402.88, mostly in cattle, real estate, and various mining claims.[9] But most of these assets had been purchased with borrowed money. The probate court allowed a $1,500 family allowance for the widow and her children. On June 8, 1896, the estate still had outstanding debts of $5,251.83. Most of the money was owed to Ronan's friends from his mining days. In 1896, $4,017.90 was owed to Henry Bratnober, who made a fortune from the Drum Lummon Mine at Marysville, near Helena, and was a hunting partner with Ronan in 1890.[10] Ronan's second large debt was $2,208.33, owed to William A. Clark, the famous Butte Copper King and Montana politician. In 1867 William and his brother, Joseph, ran a mail line between Missoula and Walla Walla, Washington, which traversed the Flathead Reservation.[11] When the Ronan estate was finally settled in 1907, interest had increased the debts to $7,211.83 with only $277.33 in cash available. The outstanding debts were settled for less than four cents on the dollar. Clearly Ronan had not grown personally rich from his position and his death left his family in straightened circumstances.

Endnotes

1. S. S. Benedict to Secretary of Interior, July 10, 1883, U.S. Department of the Interior, "Reports of Inspection of the Field Jurisdictions of the Office of Indian Affairs, 1873-1900," National Archives Microfilm Publication M1070, reel 11, Flathead Agency, 3093/1883.

2. *The Northwest Illustrated Monthly Magazine* (St. Paul, Minn.), vol. 8, no. 7 (July 1890), p. 46, col. 3.

3. P. McCormick to Secretary of Interior, Feb. 17, 1895, U.S. Department of the Interior, "Reports of Inspection of the Field Jurisdictions of the Office of Indian Affairs, 1873-1900," National Archives Microfilm Publication M1070, reel 11, Flathead Agency, 1628/1895.

4. Ronan letters, vol. 2, pp. 148-57.

5. Ronan letters, vol. 2, pp. 168-70, and 175-76.

6. "Flathead Fears," *The Helena Journal* (daily), Apr. 27, 1889, p. 1, col. 8.

7. Ronan letters, vol. 2, pp. 142-45 and 170-72.

8. There is some disagreement in the sources about the exact year of Ronan's birth. This biographical sketch was compiled from: Peter Ronan, "Discovery of Alder Gulch," *Contributions to the Historical Society of Montana,* vol. 3 (1900), pp. 143-52; "Biographical," *Missoula County Times*, Aug. 31, 1887, p. 3, col. 3; "A Montana Pioneer," *The Spokane Review*, Nov. 7, 1891, p. 3, col. 1-2; "Passed Peacefully Away," *The Evening Missoulian,* Aug. 21, 1893, p. 1, col. 5-6.

9. Estate of Peter Ronan, Probate file 339 (1893), Clerk of District Court, Missoula County Courthouse, Missoula, Mont.

10. W. Turrentine Jackson, "The Irish Fox and the British Lion," *Montana: The Magazine of Western History,* vol. 9, no. 2 (Apr. 1959), pp. 28-42; "Henry Bratnober," *The Engineering and Mining Journal,* vol. 98, no. 13 (Sept. 26, 1914), p. 579; "A Bear Story," *The New-York Times,* July 21, 1890, p. 4, col. 7.

11. *Dictionary of American Biography*, vol. 4 (1930), pp. 144-46; William D. Mangam, *The Clarks: An American* Phenomenon (New York: Silver Bow Press, 1941), pp. 32-33; Ida Smith Patterson, *Montana Memories: The Life of Emma Magee in the Rocky Mountain West, 1866-1950.* Second edition. (Pablo, Mont.: Salish Kootenai College Press, 2011), p. 22.

Biographical Glossary

Carrington, Henry B., General

Carrington had been a brigadier general of volunteers during the U.S. Civil War, in charge of raising, organizing, and training troops. He never served in combat which limited his opportunities in the regular army after 1865. Carrington's military career effectively ended on December 21, 1866, near Fort Phil Kearny, Wyoming, when he ordered Lt. Col. William J. Fetterman to assist a wood train from the fort that was under attack by Sioux, Cheyenne, and Arapaho Indians. Fetterman and the eighty other men with him fell into an ambush and were annihilated that day. Fetterman's commander, Carrington was disgraced, and he spent the rest of his life explaining and defending his actions. After being removed as commander of Fort Phil Kearny, Carrington accidentally shot himself in the thigh. He retired from the army in 1870 and developed another career as a professor of military science and an author of books and articles on military history. Carrington also became involved with the Friends of the Indians, a white Protestant movement that worked to save Indians by protecting them from white military aggression, but that also wanted to coerce them into white American cultural patterns and values.[1]

Casey, John

John Casey and Clarence Proctor were two of the most active white settlers contesting the Kootenai allotments north of the reservation boundary in 1891. The only additional information found about John Casey was that in 1890 he suffered an attack of rheumatism and went to a Yellowstone Valley hot springs for treatment.[2]

Clifford, John E.

John E. Clifford was the son-in-law of T. J. Demers, the Frenchtown merchant. Clifford's wife, Delima, was part Pend d'Oreille and educated in Montreal. In 1887 Demers put Clifford in charge of his store and other business enterprises in Demersville at the head of Flathead Lake.[3] After the killing of an unnamed Kootenai Indian by Clifford, reports of an "Indian uprising" appeared in newspapers around the nation, including the *New York Times* and *Washington Post*.[4] A Dr. Cuningham was charged as complicit in the crime. Clifford and Cuningham were brought before the grand jury for murder and discharged.[5] Later Clifford returned to operate Demers' store at Demersville.[6]

Cuningham, Dr.

This may have been Dr. Edward Francis Conyngham who was a veteran of the Confederate Army in the Civil War. He attended several medical schools in the Midwest after the war and came to Montana in the late 1880s. He was in Europe in the early 1890s and returned to Montana in 1895. He practiced medicine in the Missoula area until 1920.[7]

Dade, John, Dr.

Dr. John Dade, from Missouri, was Flathead Agency Physician between 1886 and his death in 1898. A veteran of the Mexican American War, he had been a physician in the Confederate Army during the Civil War.[8] On October 3, 1891, the Commissioner of Indian Affairs complained to Ronan that the monthly Flathead Agency sanitary or physician's reports seemed to show almost no variation from month to month. The Commissioner asked for a more detailed report from the agency physician. On November 5, 1891, the Commissioner complained that the report Ronan forwarded on October 16, 1891, was still not sufficient. On December 4, 1891, Thomas E. Adams, the agency clerk, forwarded a more detailed report to the Commissioner which was accepted.[9]

Houston, William

William Houston was elected Missoula County Sheriff in the fall of 1889 because he promised to use aggressive tactics in the hunt for Indians accused of killing white people.[10] Houston grew up in Indiana and worked on the railroad where he was involved in the pursuit and capture of several highway robbers. He also worked in the hotel business. After his 1890-1892 term as sheriff, he was a railroad employee, developer, and businessman. Houston served as police commissioner for the city of Missoula. In 1920 he was elected to a second term as Missoula County Sheriff, but after eleven months he was removed from office for incompetence and working with bootleggers.[11]

Humbert, Eugene

Eugene Humbert, who served as one of the cooks and packers on the camping trip Agent Ronan took on the reservation in 1890, came to Montana in 1863. He worked as a miner and cattleman for thirty years in western

Montana and had a business arrangement with Ronan to raise cattle on the reservation.[12]

Irvine, Robert H.

Robert H. Irvine was hired as the agency farmer for the Kootenai village in Elmo in 1890. Irvine was a mixed blood of white and Snake descent who spoke Kootenai and operated a cattle ranch on Crow Creek in the Mission Valley. Irvine had purchased $115 worth of fruit trees in 1887 and in 1891 sold his herd of 250 cattle to Alex Dow, a trader at Arlee.[13] Irvine also spoke Nez Perce and in 1877 served as interpreter during the Nez Perce War.[14] Ronan reported that in 1891, with Irvine's help, the Kootenai had done well raising wheat at Elmo. He got drunk at a Fourth of July celebration in 1891, but promised Ronan he would abstain from alcohol in the future.[15] He died at Crow Creek on February 10, 1900.[16]

Joseph Catholuha

Joseph Catholuha served as judge on the Flathead Indian court from 1888 untl his death in 1894. Joseph was eulogized by then Flathead Agent Joseph T. Carter as "wise, just and strict."[17]

Knowles, Hiram

Judge Hiram Knowles, from Maine, was a judge on the Montana Territory Supreme Court in 1878. In 1890 he was appointed to the U.S. District Court. He also spent many years in private practice.[18]

Lalasee

Lalasee, a Pend d'Oreille, was accused of murdering a white man in the Jocko Valley in 1888. According to Duncan McDonald, a mixed blood trader on the reservation, Lalasee was a family man with children and "a good Indian" before his brother was killed by white men a few years earlier. After being hunted by the reservation police and Missoula County Sheriff, Lalasee surrendered to Duncan McDonald, who escorted him to the Missoula jail. In November of that year, he was convicted of murder and was hung with three other tribal members in Missoula on December 19, 1890.[19]

Lambert, H. R.

Henry R.. Lambert was born in Minnesota and came to Montana in 1871 where he held various clerical positions in Helena until 1877 when he became "head farmer," or agency clerk, for Ronan. He worked at Flathead Agency until 1881 when he left to become a bookkeeper for a mercantile firm. In 1882 he became a partner with Alex

Demers in the store at St. Ignatius Mission. In 1884 he operated a store and hotel at the Foot of Flathead Lake (now Polson). He returned to the Flathead Agency in 1886 as farmer. Since in 1886 Ronan had an agency clerk, this time Lambert's duties were to assist tribal member farmers as well as help with the agency clerical work.[20]

LeBeau, Baptist

Baptist Le Bow or J. B. LeBeau, a French Canadian. During the 1870s LeBeau operated a flour mill in Frenchtown and also raised grain.[21] In the 1880s he raised cattle in the Flathead Valley, and in 1886 he was one of the larger taxpayers in Missoula County.[22] He died in 1907.[23]

Loughborough, Robert H. R., Lieut.

Lieutenant Robert H. R. Loughborough was from Virginia. He was promoted to major in 1900.[24]

Louis Broken Leg

According to Harry Turney-High, Louis Broken Leg was married to Eneas' daughter, Marian or "She Has Three Buckskin Dresses."[25]

Morant, Joe

Joe Morant (or Morand) was a mixed blood Indian who lived on a farm six miles north of Bigfork. He was prominent in horse racing in the area. In 1886 his horse, Grand-Jo, beat a Frenchtown horse in a big race at Ashley. Morant was killed in Missoula in a fight over a card game.[26]

Pierre Paul

Pierre Paul, a Pend d'Oreille, was accused of murdering a white man in the Jocko Valley in 1888. According to Duncan McDonald, Pierre Paul was "a rowdy and a ruffian, a desperate man with a desire to kill. The Indians were afraid of him. He was in the habit of bullying and terrorizing all with whom he came in contact, but is at heart a coward." He was hunted by the reservation tribal police and Missoula County Sheriff. In August 1890 he was captured by a posse of tribal members and taken to Missoula. In November of that year, he was convicted of murder and was hung with three other tribal members in Missoula on December 19, 1890.[27]

Powell, Israel Wood

Israel Wood Powell, a medical doctor, was Superintendent of Indian Affairs in British Columbia from 1872 through 1889. He supported limiting Indian reserves to twenty acres per family. Local British Columbia officials wanted to allow even less land.[28]

Proctor, Clarence E.

Clarence E. Proctor came to the Flathead Valley in the late 1880s. He established a hotel, livery stable, and other businesses just north of the reservation boundary. Proctor was particularly active in contesting the Kootenai allotments north of the reservation. In 1890 and 1891, he operated a real estate agency in Kalispell. Some of the available sources contradict each other about the dates of specific events in his life. He died in 1933.[29]

Ramsdell, William and Ralph

William and Ralph Ramsdell established a trading post on Tobacco Plains in 1886. Apparently, both could speak Kootenai, and Ralph even worked on a Kootenai dictionary that was never published. Ralph was part of the 1888 mob that "arrested" two Kootenai Indians accused of murdering white men. The whites lynched the Kootenais without a legal trial.[30]

In 1889 Ronan and one of the Ramsdells traded charges in the columns of *The Helena Journal*. Ramsdell listed a series of alleged murders of white people by Indians in western Montana and accused Ronan of indifference. Ronan replied that he had turned evidence of the crimes over to the United States Marshall in Helena and he charged that the Ramsdells sold liquor to Indians.[31]

In March 1890, however, William Ramsdell wrote to a local newspaper to defend Chief Eneas and the Dayton Creek Kootenai against charges that they were preparing to attack the white settlers in the Flathead Valley.[32] In 1889 William Ramsdell was elected to the Montana Constitutional Convention as a Democrat and in 1894 and in 1896 he was elected to the Montana State Senate from Flathead County as a Populist.[33]

In August 1890 Ralph was deputy sheriff in the hunt for several Kootenai accused of killing white men. In the conflict surrounding the arrests of Pascale and Antee he interpreted for Sheriff William Houston. The white lawmen held Kootenai Chief Eneas hostage for the surrender of the accused Kootenais. Ramsdell was also a leader in the posse that arrested Pierre Paul, a Pend d'Oreille. The three men were tried by a white jury, convicted along with Lalasee, and the four were hung in Missoula in December 1890.[34] Ralph Ramsdell's version of the Kootenai-white hostilities can be found in a manuscript at the Montana Historical Society Archives.[35]

Rivais, Michelle

Michel Rivais was half French and half Pend d'Oreille. A gifted linguist, he was Flathead Agency interpreter between 1877 and 1911. He could speak English, French, and a number of Indian languages. Totally blind, he was led around by his wife. He was the main source for the Salish Indian ethnography by James A. Teit.[36]

Sanborn, Washington I., Capt.

Captain Washington I. Sanborn of the 25th Infantry was born in Maine and joined the army in 1862 from Washington Territory. During a long career across the American West, he served mostly in the Pacific Northwest before retiring in 1898 as a major.[37]

Savia

Savia was the nickname of Francois Gravelle, a Frenchman from Savoy in southeastern France, who had a ranch near the Kootenai village. He was married to Eneas' niece, Elizabeth or Little Eyes, and they had five children. According to the sources, he was goodhearted and respected by both whites and Indians in the area.[38]

Sheppard, Jack

Jack Sheppard was a blacksmith at Demersville. In 1890 he was charged with cutting the throat of his father-in-law. In the subsequent divorce case he was accused of being a "habitual drunkard."[39]

Weed, Elbert D.

Elbert D. Weed, originally of New York state, came to Helena in 1883 where he practiced law. Between 1889 and 1894 he served as United States District Attorney for Montana. In 1894, he was elected mayor of Helena.[40]

Wilson, David B., Capt.

Captain David B. Wilson of Pennsylvania was a Civil War veteran. Promoted to captain in 1886, he retired as a lieutenant colonel in 1902.[41]

Endnotes

1. *The Anaconda Standard*, Nov. 1, 1889, p. 8, col. 2; "The Indian Lands," WM, Dec. 4, 1889, p. 3, col. 3; Robert J. Bigart, *Getting Good Crops: Economic and Diplomatic Survival Strategies of the Montana Bitterroot Salish Indians, 1870-1891* (Norman: University of Oklahoma Press, 2010), pp. 194-217; *Dictionary of American Biography*, vol. 3, pp. 520-21; Catherine McKeen, "Henry Beebee Carrington: A Soldier's Tale," unpublished PhD dissertation, State University of New York at Stoney Brook, 1998, DAI 9912592.

2. Ronan letters, vol. 2, pp. 225-26; Sam E. Johns, "The Pioneers," typescript, Flathead County Library, Kalispell, Mont., vol. 4, p. 176.

3. Clifford was flamboyant and popular among the white population in western Montana. In addition to his prominent business activities, Clifford was also a drinker and years later was arrested in Butte and sent to the Montana State Prison for grand larceny. Carle F. O'Neil, *Two Men of Demersville* (n.p., 1990), pp. 59-100.

4. "Unwarranted Excitement," WM, Feb. 20, 1889, p. 3, col. 4; "The Sum Total," *Missoula Gazette* (weekly), Mar. 6, 1889, p. 3, col. 3; "Flatheads Are Arming," *The New-York Times*, Feb. 21, 1889, p. 1, col. 4; "Kootenais, Not Flatheads," *The Washington Post*, Feb. 23, 1889, p. 1, col. 4.

5. "Discharged," WM, Mar. 13, 1889, p. 3, col. 5.

6. WM, Apr. 3, 1889, p. 3, col. 1.

7. Paul C. Phillips and Llwewllyn L. Callaway, *Medicine in the Making of Montana* (Missoula: Montana State University Press, 1962), pp. 420-21.

8. Paul C. Phillips, *Medicine in the Making of Montana* (Missoula: Montana Medical Association and Montana State University Press, 1962), p. 277; Missoula Publishing Company, *Flathead Facts: Descriptive of the Resources of Missoula County* (Missoula, Mont.: Missoula Publishing Company, 1890), p. 18; "Death of Dr. Dade," *Daily Democrat-Messenger* (Missoula, Mont.), Aug. 12, 1898, p. 1, col. 6; "Death of Dr. Dade," *Daily Missoulian*, Aug. 12, 1898, p. 8, col. 2-3.

9. CIA to Ronan, Oct. 3, 1891, letterbook 249, pp. 213-14, accounts; CIA to Ronan, Nov. 5, 1891, letterbook 250, pp. 399-400, accounts, NA CIA LS; Ronan letters [i.e., Thomas E. Adams], vol. 2, pp. 261-262.

10. WM, Oct. 2, 1889, p. 3, col. 3; G. M. Houtz, "Old-Time Flathead Tales: Some Modern Instances," *Daily Missoulian*, Oct. 10, 1937, p. 4, col. 2-3.

11. Bob Raffety and John C. Moe, *Sheriffs of Missoula County, Montana, and Their Times, 1860-1978* (n.p., 1988?), pp. 115-18, 169-72; Will Cave,

"Bill Houston's Story," *Daily Missoulian*, May 2, 1937, ed. sec., p. 7, col. 1-8, and May 9, 1937, ed. sec., p. 7, col. 1-8.

12. James U. Sanders, ed., *Society of Montana Pioneers,* vol. 1 (1899), p. 209; "Another Pioneer Is Called Across the Last Divide," *Daily Missoulian*, July 13, 1915, p. 8, col. 2; Estate of Peter Ronan, Probate File 339 (1893), Clerk of District Court, Missoula County Courthouse, Missoula, Mont., items 40, 43, and 47.

13. Ronan letters, v. 1, pp.401-08; *Missoula Gazette* (daily), May 5, 1891, p. 8, col. 2.

14. "Startling If True," *Helena Independent*, Aug. 5, 1877, p. 3, col. 2; "The Indian Situation," *Helena Independent*, Aug. 7, 1877, p. 3, col. 2.

15. B. H. Miller to Secretary of Interior, Dec. 15, 1891, 45,483/1891, NA CIA LR; Ronan letters, v. 2, pp. 278-79.

16. "Burial Register, 1898-1963," St. Ignatius Mission, St. Ignatius, Montana, p. 2.

17. Ronan letters, vol. 2, p. 3.

18. Joaquin Miller, *An Illustrated History of the State of Montana* (Chicago: The Lewis Publishing Co., 1894), p. 69.

19. "What Duncan Said," *Missoula Weekly Gazette*, Aug. 27, 1890, p. 5, c. 2-3; Robert Bigart and Joseph McDonald, eds., *To Keep the Land for My Children's Children: Documents of Salish, Pend d'Oreille, and Kootenai Indian History, 1890-1890* (Pablo, Mont.: Salish Kootenai College Press, 2020), pp. 33-36, 58-64.

20. Missoula Publishing Company, *Flathead Facts: Descriptive of the Resources of Missoula County* (Missoula, Mont.: Missoula Publishing Co., 1890), pp. 18-19; WM, Nov. 24, 1882, p. 3, col. 2-3; "The Flathead Country," WM, Oct. 10, 1884, p. 2, col. 1-3.

21. "To Frenchtown," WM, Nov. 10, 1875, p. 3, col. 2; WM, Oct. 18, 1878, p. 3, col. 2.

22. "Heavy Taxpayers," WM, Dec. 10, 1886, p. 2, col. 1.

23. "The Oldest Old Timer," *The Kalispell Bee,* Oct. 8, 1907, p. 3, col. 3-5; "An Old Timer Gone," *The Inter Lake* (Kalispell, Mont.), Oct. 11, 1907, p. 5, col. 4.

24. Francis B. Heitman, *Historical Register and Dictionary of the United States Army* (Washington, D.C.: U.S. Government Printing Office, 1903), vol. 1, p. 643.

25. Harry Holbert Turney-High, *Ethnography of the Kutenai,* Memoir of the American Anthropological Association No. 56 (1941), pp. 135-39.

26. Robert H. (Bob) Gatiss, *Memories of One Lifetime* (n.p., 1993), pp.

139-42.

27. "What Duncan Said," *Missoula Weekly Gazette*, Aug. 27, 1890, p. 5, c. 2-3; Robert Bigart and Joseph McDonald, eds., *To Keep the Land for My Children's Children: Documents of Salish, Pend d'Oreille, and Kootenai Indian History, 1890-1890* (Pablo, Mont.: Salish Kootenai College Press, 2020), pp. 58-64.

28, *Dictionary of Canadian Biography*, vol. 14, pp. 845-46; Robin Fisher, *Contact and Conflict: Indian-European Relations in British Columbia, 1774-1890*. Second edition. (Vancouver, B.C.: UBC Press, 1992), pp. 180-87.

29. Chief Cliff Homemakers, *Chief Cliff Country* (Dayton?, Mont.: Chief Cliff Homemakers, 1990), pp. 61-64; "C. E. Proctor & Co.," *Missoula Gazette*, Dec. 31, 1890, p. 5, col. 6; "An Embryo City," *Missoula Gazette*, Sept. 3, 1891, p. 1, col. 5-6; "Funerals," *The Daily Inter Lake* (Kalispell, Mont.), July 15, 1933, p. 3, col. 4.

30. Ogla Johnson, ed., *The Story of the Tobacco Plains Country* (Caldwell, Idaho: Pioneers of the Tobacco Plains Country, 1950), pp. 63-65, 71-73; Ronan letters, vol. 2, pp. 4-7.

31. Ronan letters, vol. 2, pp. 36-42.

32. "Unnecessary Alarm," *The Inter-Lake* (Demersville, Mont.), Mar. 7, 1890, p. 4, col. 2.

33. Ellis L. Waldron, *Montana Politics Since 1864: An Atlas of Elections* (Missoula: Montana State University Press, 1958), pp. 50, 78, 82.

34. "Cleverly Caught," *Missoula Gazette* (daily), Aug. 5, 1890, p. 1, col. 3-4; "One of Them Caught," *Missoula Gazette* (daily), Aug. 7, 1890, p. 1, col. 5; "Death's Decree," *Missoula Weekly Gazette*, Dec. 24, 1890, pp. 1-3, 5.

35. Ralph Henry Ramsdell, "Cleaning Up Northwest Montana," Ralph Henry Ramsdell reminiscences, SC 394, Montana Historical Society Archives, Helena.

36. Mary Ronan, *Girl from the Gulches: The Story of Mary Ronan*, ed. Ellen Baumler (Helena: Montana Historical Society Press, 2003), pp. 188-189; Robert J. Bigart, ed., *Life and Death at St. Mary's Mission, Montana: Births, Marriages, Deaths and Survival Among the Bitterroot Salish Indians, 1866-1891* (Pablo, Mont.: Salish Kootenai College Press, 2005), pp. 320-21; "Michel Revais' Life Ends After Many Useful Years of Service of Government," *The Daily Missoulian*, Jan. 15, 1911, p. 1, c. 3-5.

37. William H. Powell, *Powell's Records of Living Officers of the United States Army* (Philadelphia, Penna.: L. R. Hamersly & Co., 1890), p. 519; Francis B. Heitman, *Historical Register and Dictionary of the United States Army* (Washington D.C.: U.S. Government Printing Office, 1903), vol. 1, p. 858.

38. Robert Bigart and Clarence Woodcock, editors, "St. Ignatius Mission, Montana: Reports from Two Jesuit Missionaries, 1885 & 1900-1901 (Part I)," *Arizona and the West,* vol. 23, no. 2 (Summer 1981), pp. 163-64; Andrew W. Swaney, "Statement of Andrew W. Swaney," Henry Elwood Papers, MC 309, box 4, folder 26, Montana Historical Society Archives, Helena, pp. 4-5.

39. "The Beautiful Lake Country," *Missoula Gazette,* May 26, 1888, p. 4, col. 1-2; *Missoula Daily Gazette,* Feb. 22, 1890, p. 8, col. 2; "Jangled Bells," *Missoula Daily Gazette,* Feb. 26, 1890, p. 4, col. 2.

40. Joaquin Miller, *An Illustrated History of the State of Montana* (Chicago: The Lewis Publishing Co., 1894), pp. 118-19.

41. William H. Powell, *Powell's Records of Living Officers of the United States Army* (Philadelphia: L. R. Hamserly & Co., 1890), pp. 650-51; Francis B. Heitman, *Historical Register and Dictionary of the United States Army* (Washington, D.C.: U.S. Government Printing Office, 1903), vol. 1, p. 1045.

Abbreviations Used in Footnotes

CIA — Commissioner of Indian Affairs

NA — National Archives, Washington, D.C.

NA CIA LR — Letters Received, Records of the Commissioner of Indian Affairs, RG 75, National Archives, Washington, D.C.

NA CIA LS — Letters Sent, Records of the Commissioner of Indian Affairs, RG 75, National Archives, Washington, D.C.

NAmf — National Archives Microfilm Publication

Ronan letters, vol. 1 — Peter Ronan, *"A Great Many of Us Have Good Farms": Agent Peter Ronan Reports on the Flathead Indian Reservation, 1877-1887,* ed. Robert J. Bigart (Pablo, Mont.: Salish Kootenai College Press, 2014)

Ronan letters, vol. 2 — Peter Ronan, *Justice to Be Accorded to the Indians: Agent Peter Ronan Reports on the Flathead Indian Reservation, 1888-1893*, ed. Robert J. Bigart (Pablo, Mont.: Salish Kootenai College Press, 2014)

WM — *The Weekly Missoulian*

Index